CARIBBEAN
HIDEAWAYS

CARIBBEAN HIDEAWAYS

Discovering Enchanting Rooms and Private Villas

Meg Nolan van Reesema

photography by
Jessica Antola

RIZZOLI
NEW YORK

First published in the United States of America in 2010
by Rizzoli International Publications, Inc.
300 Park Avenue South
New York, NY 10010
www.rizzoliusa.com

2010   2011   2012   2013   /   10   9   8   7   6   5   4   3   2   1

Distributed in the U.S. trade by Random House, New York

Printed in Singapore

ISBN-13: 978-0-8478-3292-7

Library of Congress Catalog Control Number: 2010927251

MARQUIS JET
fleet by NetJets

TITLE PAGE *The beloved, palm-framed main drive at Tryall.*

CONTENTS

FOREWORD

....

CHRIS BLACKWELL

*O*nce the center of the world, the Caribbean islands were thriving international ports directing global commerce, exporting some of the most precious natural resources, and even encouraging territorial battles on a regular basis. And, of course, giving birth to the original rebels: pirates. Today, the intoxicating essence of the Caribbean—the colors, smells, people, and most obviously, the natural beauty—continues to command a universal pull on the rest of the world, and yes, still creates modern-day misfits like myself. Jamaica, my childhood home, was hugely influential in its heyday and retains its powerful and emblematic culture, attracting outsiders and inspiring natives, like myself, to employ dynamic ways to showcase it.

Despite the years I spent in England, I never quite left Jamaica, and when I did, it usually came with me. Growing up in Jamaica I did different things. I rented motor scooters. I had a little jazz club and I managed sixty-three jukeboxes, which meant I had to go all around the country, any place that had my jukeboxes, to change the records and argue about the availability of the requisite three-penny pieces with the owner of a bar in a little fishing village or up in the hills. It was all great stuff to absorb—real life.

Perhaps the collective compulsion for the island experience—the core reason behind people arriving in droves, day after day—is the opportunity for direct communication with nature. Here in Jamaica, with its lush Blue Mountains, the opportunity is especially evident. In order to preserve that distinct bond, a strong commitment to nature must be made, particularly in partnership with new development. I'd always rather build around a tree than cut one down.

In Meg Nolan van Reesema's book *Caribbean Hideaways*, the Caribbean's natural beauty is on full display, if not enhanced by her selection of exceptional properties that have been chosen to provide equally alluring interiors within their lush environments. Fortunately she discovered a bounty of spots in Jamaica—by far it has the majority of any of the other islands. I'm pleased that *Goldeneye* is included among them and moreover, that the sense of enchantment and authenticity I look to offer is recognizable to others.

I invite you all to come see for yourself soon.

*The lush foliage and natural style
of Goldeneye's discreet setting.*

INTRODUCTION

My first trip to the Caribbean was ideally timed. At twelve I was just old enough to appreciate the exotic island culture, but still young enough to feel giddy over the white sand and vivid ocean color. Now, eighteen years later, my family and I continue to make the annual pilgrimage down to Jamaica, to the very same beloved family resort, the Tryall Club, a former hideaway just west of Montego Bay. And although the sight of aqua-blue waters has become less shocking over the years, my anticipation for the Jamaica vacation has only intensified.

Hunting for enchanting rooms and villa hideaways in the Caribbean was a delicious assignment, though not without challenge. If there was one thing I learned throughout my travels in the islands it was that each structure, no matter its size or luxurious materials, is at constant battle with nature. The moisture-laden weather, the jungle-like plant life, and the multitude of insects and birds can wreak havoc on buildings and especially interiors. However, this bleak truth only served to make the selections included here even more exceptional. Despite the common clash with the elements, these thirty hideaways have utilized creative design techniques to ensure their properties are as inspirational and welcoming as the landscape of the islands themselves.

Having stayed in hundreds of hotels and resorts these past few years, I maintain an unwavering allegiance I feel towards Tryall. It is due in part to the fact that Tryall was relatively unknown when my family first ventured there in 1992, allowing us the intoxicating element of discovery. It felt like our own treasure island and inspired the fierce loyalty we feel today. The other parts can be easily explained by the consistency of our visits, our cherished group of friends and the countless, precious memories (not to mention, birthday celebrations) that have transpired over the years.

However, Tryall also deserves credit. With its personal, family-oriented setup and decidedly unstuffy atmosphere, guests acquire a a sense of familiarity with the spot even upon the first few days of the initial visit. The majority of the guests stay in fully staffed villas where they are the architects of their pleasure, choosing everything from the daily meals prepared by the private chef to whether they'd like cocktail hour to begin at 5 P.M. or noon. The constant interaction with the staff, some of whom live on site, allows for wonderful personal relationships to develop, enriching the Tryall experience tenfold. The staff at our beloved EveSong villa have become extended family members.

Another credit to Tryall's design is the simple fact that most of the meals are taken in the privacy of the guest villas, providing you and your companions optimal time together. My parents relished this, having children widely spaced in age who had gone off to school at different times. The annual Tryall vacation offered guaranteed quality family time. What strikes me most about Tryall though, is that the loyalty I feel is felt equally among each individual in my family and our group of "Tryall friends." I'll never forget when during my first year away at school I suffered a bout of homesickness and my closest friend and Tryall-pal, Hayden, consoled me with the words, "Don't

ABOVE, FROM LEFT TO RIGHT
The commanding hilltop position of Tryall's great house; the colonial stone entrance of the great house.

FOLLOWING PAGES   *The seaside pool at the villa, Reef House, owned by the vivacious Annie Nickel Curtin.*

worry, we'll soon be at Tryall, where the nighttime sounds of the tree frogs will lull you to sleep and make it all better." I am fairly certain those words would console me still today.

Although Tryall has developed over the years and grown far beyond its original hideaway status when the Great House Bar was porch-less and the Commissary was lucky to carry red wine, my devotion remains intact. So much so, that I wish everyone a similar discovery, a hideaway among the palm trees, whose specialness brings recurring enjoyment.

MEG NOLAN VAN REESEMA
March 2009

BIRD OF PARADISE VILLA

ANGUILLA, WEST INDIES

*T*he sixteen-mile-long island of Anguilla looks like an impressive sandbar from the air, albeit with various construction sites and sprawling whitewashed resorts. Absent of the lush green hills that characterize other islands, Anguilla nevertheless reveals equal allure through its flat, sandy stretch and translucent aqua-blue waters. Undeniably the Caribbean island with the best walking

beaches—the expanses of powder-fine sand feel deliciously soft between your toes—Anguilla is a haven for beach lovers and sun worshippers. Basking in the shadow of its neighbor, the mountainous St. Martin, Anguilla feels every bit the castaway island with thirty-three different beaches, fiery flamboyant trees, wandering goats (arguably Anguilla's national animal), and enough beach bars to ensure a rum-soaked game of dominoes or steel-drum accented music is never difficult to find.

Like a golden crown, the 10,500-square-foot custom-designed Bird of Paradise villa sits atop one of Anguilla's most dramatic elevations, Sandy Hill, overlooking the bay with St. Barths and St. Martin in the distance. Designed by architect Guy Courtney of the lauded Wilson Associates, the Dallas architecture firm whose credits include the Four Seasons in Hawaii, Atlantis in the Bahamas, and Las Ventanas in Cabo San Lucas, this Southeast Asian tropical–style villa is a testament to the successful combination of high-minded homeowners and a prized professional. After seeing the architecture firm's work at Fregate Island in the Seychelles, industrious owners Melody and Jon Dill contacted them on the off chance they might be interested in a residential project. If any-

thing teaches a person to reach for the stars, Melody Dill's custom, uberluxe four-bedroom villa with lagoon-style pools, sunken veranda with trellises, and outdoor fireplace certainly does. A true labor of love and fastidious planning, the Bird of Paradise came together through the careful toil of Melody and interior designer Tonya Burke. Leafing through Melody's carefully organized binders of blueprints, interior sketches, furniture orders, and fabric samples is enough to ignite schoolgirl envy. Every detail is documented, from the trim on the pillows of the master bedroom's porch to the extra-heavy Balinese hurricanes on the dining room table. Perhaps the most fascinating element (and equally well documented in its own separate brief available to guests) is the extensive collection of indigenous artifacts displayed throughout the house. All of them were collected during the Dills' exotic travels in Southeast Asia and Africa (including a carved, life-size Indonesian love god). Avid travelers, the Dills count Papua New Guinea as one of their favorite spots and thus chose its rare and beautiful bird species—the bird-of-paradise—as the villa's namesake. Furthermore, the Dills are generous, involved owners, intent on ensuring your stay runs as smoothly as possible and that you enjoy

their villa, and island, as much as they do. Do not hesitate to ask them even the smallest request.

In a similar fashion to a luxury hotel's villa, the Bird, as it is affectionately known, features top-drawer amenities, from Frette linens and robes to Bulgari toiletries and multiple flat-screen HDTVs. The Bird also boasts a private chef, Zoe, who is available on either a meal-to -meal or all-inclusive plan. A native Californian, Zoe was trained in France and has been on Anguilla for fifteen years, first running a small restaurant and now cooking exclusively for the Bird's lucky guests. Every dish, from eggs Benedict and raspberry coffee cake in the morning to lobster salad at lunch, is homemade. Zoe's cooking is so consistently delicious that you'll find yourself shocked when you return home and realize the enormity of how well you've just-been eating despite the seemingly simple presentation. Meals are served either on the long teak dining table on the veranda, the round kitchen table, or on special occasions, smack in the center foyer with the lagoon pool's LED light show creating the mood. Table settings include Balinese place mats and specially commissioned, emerald-colored china while the chair cushions and napkins are Jim Thompson's colorful Thai silk fabrics. The indoor-outdoor flow of the Bird's design allows the days to lazily slip away as you meander from one cushioned spot to another. Whether it's on the Indonesian *bale*, or daybed—correctly positioned according to Indonesian tradition at the entrance of the house—or in the reclined plantation chairs on the veranda, or in the teak deck chairs off the guest room's individual terraces, locations for lounging with a good book or catnapping are widely abundant. Given the villa's exposed hilltop location, the Christmas winds (which seem to last into early February) can be quite strong; fortunately the villa's designers installed a stylish jatoba-wood screen on one side of the veranda to protect the dining table and brush bottoms on all the screen doors so they don't bang in the wind. If the weather proves inclement or the sun too strong, the richly appointed colonial-style living room with coumarou vaulted ceilings, cove lighting that can be dimmed, folding glass doors framed in mahogany, and pastel fabric pillows from Raoul Textiles, Duralee, and Hargett makes for quite an elegant shelter. Furnishings like the carved Madura coffee table from John Erdos, the custom teak side tables from Bali, and the simple rattan sofa from Bauer lend a soothing, neutral tone to the eclectic details like the copper bird from Borneo, the colonial-style ottomans, and silver lamps from Uttermost. The concerted mixture of name-brand furnishings, custom Asian imports, and artistic collectibles give the room an unpretentious feel while remaining elegantly composed. The Bird of Paradise strikes that elusive balance of being both full of distinct character and yet widely appealing.

ROOMS

The four bedrooms of the Bird of Paradise are set on three different elevations and are generously spaced around and below the main building. The master suite is tucked off to the right, shrouded by palms and connected to the main building by a small Balinese footbridge over the lagoon pool, and marked at the entry with a wall carving from Borneo featuring birds-of-paradise. Befitting a master, the suite has a large separate bathroom with Jacuzzi tub and walk-in vanity area. The walls are hand finished in beige plaster and the four-poster Madura bed, teeming with cream-colored linen pillows from Bergamo, looks out through a set of French doors over a small dipping pool to the sparkling sea and distant outline of St. Barths. Despite the master suite's detached location, the suite with the most privacy is the guest room below the main building, accessible by a set of stairs off the outdoor living room. Secluded on its very own level with a crescent-shaped stone terrace that seems to jut out over the water, the lower guest room is the preferred room for a hideaway stay. The four-poster queen-size bed is littered with linen pillows in robin's-egg blue from Raoul Textiles and Morella. A Balinese wall carving hangs over the head of the bed while silver necklaces brought back from the Dills' trip to East Africa adorn the other wall. The two sets of French doors have separate screen doors, ideal for filtering the bugs and breeze while sleeping with the sounds of the sea. The room's separate bar area with a premium coffeemaker and stocked minifridge is a hotel-style delight, as are the spacious closets with shelves, cloth-lined rattan drawers, and even a minisafe. The stone-tile floor and shower, brushed-nickel fixtures from Kohler, and amber-colored granite counters give the bathroom a desert appeal, while the simple cream walls and teak doorframes keep the room rooted in a neutral palette. The third and fourth bedrooms are stacked on top of each other in the same building on the opposite side of the main house than the master. The upper-level suite features a wall of sliding doors directly in front of the bed that retract completely to unveil the eastern-facing view—bliss for early risers. A sitting room in the back doubles both as an office with a flat-screen television and a separate entrance to the outdoor living room. The sofa can be made up for nannies or is a perfect spot for small children to nap or watch a DVD. The lower suite has two double beds and an impressive collection of woven baskets, carved masks, and tapestries from Africa adorning the walls, making it easily the most ornamented room in the house. Each of the suites has both ceiling fans and air-conditioning (should the island breeze be insufficient) along with Wi-Fi in case the outside world must encroach. The small beach below is just a two-minute walk down a cut path, and though not quite long enough for a real jog, it provides a nice cove for quick swims or a short strolls. The beach is also quite empty, used only by the three other neighboring villas. Although other beaches on the island have far smoother sand, the convenience and privacy are easily appreciated (particularly at night or dawn).

CLOCKWISE FROM TOP LEFT   *The moat-like pool separates the master bedroom; original West Papuan artifacts in the guest room; an authentic Indonesian daybed located, customarily, by the villa's front entrance; the robin's-egg-blue palette in the deluxe guest room.*

Cozy teak lounge chairs overlooking the sea and the island of Saint Barth's in the distance.

HERMITAGE BAY

ANTIGUA

*D*riving down the unpaved road to Hermitage Bay seems a significant detour in Antigua—a Caribbean island whose relative wealth is apparent right from the airport. The absence of signage, plus the road's deep potholes, push the idea of "off the beaten track" to its full meaning while the lusciously verdant, hilly landscape promotes an ensconced feeling. But pulling into the gravel driveway, passing hedgerows of hibiscus and allamanda and the eight alluring beach bungalows of Hermitage Bay, turn those bumps into a distant memory. The open-air, Balinese-inspired reception building continues the soothing transition with dark wood floors, black rattan sofas, and cream-and-brown linen cushions. The walls are covered in framed photographs of a young Bob Marley shot in candid poses by a former girlfriend. The owners of the hotel, one a Brit and the other Jamaican, clearly understand the power of these images and the soothing mood they evoke—one that is re-emphasized when the guest is presented with a cool towel and a refreshing virgin mojito. Reminiscent of a rambling beach house, the ranch-style building expands out to either side and fronts white sand and aquamarine bay.

A popular spot with Europeans (particularly Italians), the resort and its activities seem to best appease those happy to just lounge. Most guests laze their days away either on the beach or poolside. The adorable attendants promptly prepare your chair as you walk toward the beach with not one but two towels, and then deliver an ice bucket filled with four bottles of icy-cold water, as well as a plate of fresh fruit. They're also at your disposal for any other drink or food needs throughout the day. I must recommend a late-morning caffè shakerato—an Italian ice-coffee drink that the bartender whipped up without explanation. Despite the overwhelmingly relaxed atmosphere, the beach does have an activities shack that offers two Hobie Cat sailboats and kayaks. The quarter-mile beach allows for a nice stroll while its crescent shape keeps the bay calm and protected—not to mention invitingly warm. There's also an island just across the bay that makes for a great kayaking destination as well as a private picnic spot, a treat the hotel will gladly set up for you. A darling gift shop is tucked alongside the main lobby and stocked with attractive bathing suits, European skin creams, and native island jewelry.

The one and only restaurant wisely offers numerous seating options, including an elevated deck and an outdoor patio, so that meals can feel a bit different as the day goes on. Given that the resort is all-inclusive, the need for consistently well-prepared food is a must. Fortunately, the menu, which changes daily, is also way above the Caribbean average, with homemade fruit yogurts and pancakes, large fresh salads with local produce, and sophisticated entrées like duck with plantains followed by decadent desserts such as molten lava chocolate cake. Newly organized cooking classes will also allow you to attempt to recreate your favorite dishes at home. The wine selection may be the only disappointment, but if you're willing to pay more for the reserves, then there are some decent options. In the evening, a reggae or jazz band serenades at cocktail hour, encouraging moonlit dancing on the pool deck.

ROOMS

The twenty-five cottages of Hermitage Bay are equal in size and offering, but as in any typical hotel, some have better views and more pleasing configurations. The first distinction is between the eight beach cottage suites and the seventeen slightly larger hillside cottages surrounded by bougainvillea. For ultimate privacy, I suggest the cottages on either end of the three rows on the hill—rooms 39, 31, and 34. If it's beachfront you desire, then numbers 1 through 4 are the preferred choices. Before you book, it is worth asking the hotel whether a neighboring cottage will be occupied, given the close proximity of some of the cottages. My favorite is hillside cottage number 25, with its bright pink hibiscus bushes and multifaceted view of the bay, the salt ponds, and the neighboring harbor, not to mention its relatively short stroll to the beach. From its privileged position, cottage 25 also enjoys direct sunset views, particularly in the fall months when the sun sets right between the two small hills beyond, as well as the whispering lullaby of crashing waves at night. Like all the rooms available at Hermitage Bay, the cottage features a spacious outdoor shower, a roll-top tub, and square-shaped

dip pools. The open-air layout is created with full-length folding doors (with screens!) and generous wraparound porches offering constant access to the 180-degree views. The dipping pools come equipped with chaise longues, though the cushioned benches with flowing muslin curtains are the preferred, if not more island-appropriate, spot to repose and soak in the tropical landscape. The hillside cottages tend to take on more of a tree-house feel, given the surrounding flora and fauna, but every one of the cottages exudes an island-bungalow style with wood-beamed ceilings, bamboo-adorned closet doors, and refreshingly minimal decoration. The interior of the rooms is decidedly contemporary with espresso-colored bed

frames, violet-trimmed cotton linens, and stark white walls. The few actual windows and walls of sliding doors are louvered and mosquito netting hangs loosely from the ceiling, setting the tone for a barefoot, nonfussy atmosphere. And while air-conditioning, flat-screen televisions, and DVD players are in the room, the ceiling fan, warm breezes, and the view are all far more alluring. However, iPod docks with surround-sound speakers (including one over the tub) make packing your iPod a must. The bathrooms are surprisingly modern and chic with double vanities and square sink basins. The hillside cottages can get a bit buggy on a still night so be sure to use the citronella coils they provide and equip yourself with some bug spray. The per-

sonalized contents of the minibar and the Illy coffee with a French press make long lazy mornings inevitable.

The most impressive aspect of Hermitage Bay is its promise—and delivery—of tranquility. The serene setting, well-equipped cottages, uncomplicated décor, and commendable cuisine together form the ideal cocktail of chilled-out bliss. And if that's not enough, a small spa, nestled in the low part of the hillside, offers complimentary welcome massages to all guests plus seven signature Dorissima color aromatherapy treatments. A top spot for honeymooners or the increasingly popular "babymooners," Hermitage Bay and its secluded location offer a relatively untrodden path to paradise.

Bright bougainvillea bushes lead the way to the hillside cottages.

CLOCKWISE FROM TOP LEFT *A secluded hillside cottage complete with dip pool; Cinderella's soaking tub with a sparkling view and singing visitor; bamboo walls found in the lobby; Balinese-inspired furnishings near the restaurant.*

FOLLOWING PAGES *The serene beachfront at Hermitage Bay.*

COBBLERS COVE

BARBADOS

The small, painted sign of Cobblers Cove swings on its hinges as cars whiz by along the main road between Speightstown and Holetown, on the popular western coast of Barbados. Yet once you pull into the tight front driveway, a high stone wall, leafy palms, and pink bougainvillea bushes provide ample barrier from the road, inviting you into the lush, three-acre garden property. Set

up in a similar way to an English country house (after all, Barbados is by far the most English island in the Caribbean), Cobblers Cove is intimately laid out with a turret-adorned main house at the center and ten two-story guest bungalows fanning out from its sides. While the former plantation house's light pink façade, white-trimmed turrets, and louvered windows conjure images of Lilly Pulitzer and knee sock–clad visitors, its guests can be seen, instead, casually milling around in sarongs or even dripping wet, direct from the pool or sea. The setting is purposely congenial and guests are often found chatting to one another over the tropical hedgerows that separate the front sitting areas of each of the ground-floor rooms. The property is beloved by its guests (it has a ninety-five percent return rate), many coming back again and again for over twenty-five years. Situated on a flat piece of private beachfront land and shaded by manicured gardens, the hotel feels every bit the respite from the busy world beyond. A small spa, gift shop, and library help the property feel all encompassing, while a tennis court and gym, plus an arts-and-crafts room for children, provide the guests with various options for activities. My favorite spot, though, is the hotel's mahogany and sky-blue leather-trimmed bar overlooking the sea,

pool, and the Terrace Restaurant, located just off the attractively decorated interior lounge. As if one has walked through a time warp back to the early 1960s, the bar is surrounded by white-painted bar stools and sets of high-back rattan swivel chairs with kitschy blue-and-white polka-dot print cushions. The amiable bartenders, each dressed in a pressed pink shirt adorned with a small Relais & Châteaux gold fleur-de-lis pin, cheerfully steer you toward either the signature "Cobblers Cove," a frightfully strong rum-and-fruit-juice concoction or one of their own creations, complete with floral embellishments. (Virgil's specialty, the "Virgil Teaser," is deadly delicious with hints of banana and melon liquor.) The traditional style décor of the main house and bar, including the crisp English fabrics, bright red porcelain lamps, and woven straw carpet in the lounge is a welcome contradiction to the dark teak furnishings that dominate Caribbean spots today. Whitewashed walls, a Messel green wrought-iron banister, and terra-cotta tile flooring lend a formal elegance to the main house that's neither stuffy nor outdated. Instead, the high ceilings, framed map prints, and see-through view to the aqua-blue sea induce a sincere relaxation that comes only when one is truly comfortable in her surroundings.

The country-club feel of the small property, which is almost camplike, particularly given the guest room architecture, is especially evident at mealtime when guests gather en masse. Breakfast tends to be ordered to the room or at the Terrace Restaurant, then lunch at the Terrace or under the few umbrella tables on the pool's brick deck, but dinner is always at the Terrace, which dresses up quite elegantly at night with fine linen and china. Furthermore, the fare is also similar to what can be found at country clubs. For lunch, the blackened shrimp or chicken Caesar salad is a staple favorite. Dinner, though, is a true highlight, with entrées such as grilled cou cou (a local fish) and linguine with rock lobster, shrimp, and scallops. The restaurant is popular with patrons from beyond the resort but given its own guests' regular attendance, outside reservations can be hard to come by. At Cobblers Cove the crowd tends to drift into a seemingly programmed sequence: from mornings on the lounge chairs by the pool overlooking the beach (follow others by saving your preferred seats with your towel and book before breakfast) to shaded afternoons reading on your room's balcony or grass terrace, to daily tea, casually presented under the lounge's screened gazebo with a varied selection of cookies, cakes, and pastries—rightly within the English-Carribean tradition. The pace is determinedly slow at Cobblers Cove (particularly in January and February when the average age of guests is sixty-eight and no children under twelve are allowed) and the emphasis is on relaxation. If exercise is essential to you, rest assured you'll be able to get time on the

PREVIOUS PAGES *The waterfront restaurant terrace.*

OPPOSITE PAGE *The Bajan Pink clubhouse sets the classic, colonial tone.*

BELOW *A room with a view—the Colleton Suite*

tennis court or on whichever machine you desire in the small gym. Cobblers Cove's central location on the western coast is also ideal for exploring Barbados. From playing the estimable Sandy Lane golf courses to dining out—Barbados is the only Caribbean island with a Zagat guide—to seeing live reggae in Speightstown, or shopping and barhopping in Holetown, the many sights of Barbados will easily fill a week. However, you'll be hard-pressed to leave Cobblers Cove during sunset, when the pink light bathes the entire property and you can guarantee a front-row seat from just about anywhere.

ROOMS

The forty suites at Cobblers Cove are dispersed among twenty, double-story bungalows painted white and green and shaded by large traveler's palms. Laid out in identical fashion, the comfortable tiled-floor suites feature front sitting rooms with cushy sofas, kitchenettes with stocked minibars, and walk-in closets with petite vanities. Undeniably old-fashioned, the rooms feature Bajan-made wicker furniture and fabrics in tropical colors mixed with simple white cushions and paintings of island life. The rooms offer beachside simplicity, allowing the outdoors to retain the majority of splendor. I prefer the second-floor rooms with their balconies' elevated privacy for lounging or enjoying breakfast. I recommend rooms 2 and 4 for their ocean views, though the blue-and-white fabric in room 8 is a charming alternative. The bathrooms in the suites are a tad tired and could use a little sprucing, along with the beds, whose pushed-together

twin mattresses and low height cater to the elderly far too pointedly. Nevertheless, the suites are clean and spacious and, given the easygoing ambience at the Cove, there's little need for modern-day amenities like flat-screen televisions and rain showers (of which there are neither). Mercifully, air-conditioning and Wi-Fi are available to ensure not all contemporary comforts have been overlooked. For those less inclined to the less appointed, there are the Colleton and Camelot suites, regally situated on the second floor of the main house. Decorated by renowned English designer Prue Lane Fox, each suite occupies one of the two turrets and features panoramic sea views, a private terrace (one suite with a plunge pool and the other with a hot tub), and the delicious exclusivity of location and convenience. The 1,780-square-foot Colleton suite is my preference among the two. Its palm tree, Colefax and Fowler chintz, empress-size four-poster bed, and sisal area rugs laid over cool marble floors are all soothing elements confirming the elegant comfort of the room. Split into, three rooms—the bedroom, sitting room and walk-in dressing area and bathroom—the suite has plenty of space. The bedroom's horseshoe shape (due to the turret's architecture) fulfills childhood fantasies of sleeping in a castle, while the view of blue sky, turquoise water, and palm leaves satisfies adulthood's tropical daydreams. Through two sets of French doors lies the sizable terra-cotta terrace with its uninterrupted sunset view (even from within the plunge pool) and whimsical mural on the back wall, depicting the history of the Colleton family in Barbados. The carrara marble bathroom

and separate dressing area with Messel green vanity are what sold me on the suite. It's no wonder that the robes were clearly thought-out—done in a blue-and-white striped seersucker with sharp navy trim, you may never get out of yours during your entire stay. The signature suites are clearly well suited to honeymooners, though those who wish to stay for "the season" and privately entertain can utilize the large sitting room and six-person dining table of the Colleton suite. Heralded as two of the top suites in the Caribbean, the Colleton and the Camelot are rarely available due to returning guests—some of whom have even fostered friendships over the years. But even if one of those rooms is available for just one night during your stay, take it—it's a memorable splurge.

CLOCKWISE FROM TOP LEFT *A country, English palette of whites and greens in the 1,780 square-foot, Colleton suite; an Oliver Messel green dressing table in the Colleton suite; a second-floor suite's shaded terrace; marble floors and white furnishings in the sitting room of the Colleton Suite.*

The Colleton suite's cushy couch calls for a good book.

FUSTIC HOUSE

BARBADOS

*J*ust past the final curve heading north on the western coastal road, down a small, local lane, stand the imposing stone pillars and automated gate of the elegant private estate, Fustic House. Pronounced *fuh-stick* by the Bajans, the seventeenth-century estate is set on eleven acres of carefully tended gardens. Despite the loss of the surrounding plantation, the original great house maintains

its graceful air, having been redesigned in the 1970s by renowned theatrical designer Oliver Messel and set among gardens designed by Todd Longstaffe-Gowan. The noted open-air style of Messel is on heavy display at Fustic House, along with his signature shade of green adorning the shutters, iron furniture, and window frames. Currently owned by Englishman William Gordon and his Russian wife, Usha, the six-bedroom house, while painstakingly updated and personalized, remains every bit a testament to colonial island living. The long gravel driveway and the curved stone walls of the entrance are overwhelmed with tropical foliage and moss, giving arrivals a mysterious aura, while two identical empress-green benches flank the front path, hinting at the sophistication inside. From its hilltop position, the house has commanding western-facing views of the sea as well as the small tin-roof houses of the fishing village of Half Moon Fort below, yet no view is without interruption from the abundance of tall bamboo plants, frangipani, African tulip, royal palms, Norfolk pine, and mahogany trees. The property is so lush and fertile (an impressive orchid garden lies on the level below the courtyard) that the landscape requires daily maintenance by four full-time gardeners. As they say in the islands, every

day is a battle with the elements, yet it appears to be a labor of love at Fustic House. For a visitor, it was absolute bliss to feel so totally enveloped in the greenery and gardens and discover clearings like a small, scenic point with a cushioned bench, a meditation gazebo tucked along the ravine, and even a Messel-designed lagoon pool carved into the rocks—all of them secret treasures. It's hard to walk the grounds at Fustic House and not imagine the most fabulous party, particularly in the central stone courtyard with its antique iron furniture and canopy trees strewn with twinkle lights.

The classic stone architecture and layout of the house, with its arched doorways, louvered shutters, and iron balconies, declare refinement amidst a casual layout. Separated into three different wings and one pavilion, Fustic House features seven double bedrooms, all with en suite bathrooms, making it easy for either friends or a large family to take over. The generous spacing between the wings and their suites ensure privacy plus a comfortable distance from one another, should it be desirable. The two central wings create an L shape around the stone courtyard and are connected by a second-story terrace walkway. The main wing is a hub of activity, featuring the library, living room, dining room, kitchen, and master bedroom suite. The light-filled

living room is accessed from two staircases, one the original seventeenth-century stone entryway and the other, wooden steps from the central courtyard. The multiple entrances, long terraces, and various staircases are elemental to the design and flow of the house. The outside is always accessible and nothing is kept shuttered in. The interiors are decorated with such deference to the surrounding environment that it feels incongruous (though instantly appreciated) to find a beautiful antique desk, flat-screen television, and shelves in the library filled to the brim with William's enviable music collection. The sets of louvered French doors and Georgian-sized windows are perpetually open to the breeze, making the rooms feel more like cozy spots in the shade than real interior spaces. Of course, air-conditioning is provided in every room if the weather turns muggy. The tangential wing, the Messel Wing as it is called, has three bedrooms and my favorite room (if you can even call it a room) on the property. Set up masterfully by the enchanting, wisteria-covered façade of the front entrance, the open-air parlor immediately charms the first-time visitor. Its brushed limestone floors, stone pillars, and roman arches open on one side to the courtyard and to the glittering sea view on the other. The classical architecture creates an ambience of prominent distinction while the casual wicker and slip-covered furnishings counter with a relaxed tone. Potted orchids and flickering votives serve as fresh accents to the enduring architecture. Absent of decorative fanfare (a few family photos and glass lamps aside) the décor of Fustic House's main rooms is presented in

PREVIOUS PAGES *The wisteria-laden entry of Fustic House.*

ABOVE, FROM LEFT TO RIGHT *Oliver Messel's lush lagoon pool design; the etched stone plaque announcing the estate.*

OPPOSITE PAGE *Twinkling lights add to the ambiance of the Fustic House's stone courtyard.*

understated harmony to the splendor of the house's classic structure and the monochrome color green.

Perhaps the most indulgent part of being a guest at Fustic House is the incredible service and staff. With fifteen staff members, plus their full-time chef, Kenroy, and affable butler, Neil, the only thing a guest must do is ask. Property manager and former lieutenant in the British army, Tony will customize your visit, including a VIP greeting at customs with optional helicopter transfer to nearby Port St. Charles, tee-times, surf lessons, four-wheel drive excursions, polo match tickets, and simple dining reservations. Staying at the estate also has luxury trimmings like a complimentary membership to the Port St. Charles marina just down the road, its waterfront dining area, pool, beaches, and billiards room offering a more social alternative— though you'd be hard-pressed to exceed the luxury of Fustic House's lunch set up under the mahogany trees in the garden or the four-course dinners under the twinkling chandelier in the courtyard. Despite Kenroy's high-cuisine triumphs at dinner and the diet-busting omelets and pastries each morning, lunch at Fustic, with its picturesque alfresco locations,

crisp rosé wine, and fresh seafood pastas or homemade vegetable quiches, was my favorite meal (and event) of day. I can still smell the fresh basil in the pasta and feel the cool breeze billowing the table's floral cloth while I decadently twiddled my toes through the grass and scanned the trees for the Bajan green monkeys that paid daily visits to the treetops.

ROOMS

The seven suites of Fustic House are spread out among four different buildings. Each feature a king-size bed or double queen-size beds and recently renovated bathrooms en suite. The guest rooms in the two front wings, including the Master suite, are done in a fresh white-and-Messel-green palette with painted wood floors, louvered windows, and French doors open to the balcony. The two guest rooms in the Plantation wing, farther afield, are my favorite, given their added privacy, spacious dimensions, and stone-walled outdoor showers. The Mahogany suite is suitably named for its regal four-poster bed and antique dresser, as well as its charming vanity in the bathroom. Both of the rooms have multiple French doors that

open to the gardens and the extended veranda littered with chaise longues and wicker sofas. There's also a Ping-Pong table in the foyer of the wing awaiting the young (and old) revelers plus a trampoline located toward the back of the yard closest to the Plantation wing, claiming exercise benefits yet also another fun pursuit. The latest addition to the estate is the new Pavilion suite at the bottom of the property's ravine and closest to the small village and beach. The multipurpose room and adjoining guest room feature a sixty-inch plasma television with a Blu-ray DVD player and a Martin Logan electrostatic-speaker sound system, definitively making it the most modern area of the estate. Staying at Fustic House has a unique type of privilege to it. The exceptional quality and nature of the estate increases with each hour spent on property and seemingly doubles with every re-entrance through the ancient stone pillars and green gate. Although modern luxuries abound at the property and no guest's need will ever go unfulfilled, the essence of Fustic House, the indescribable aura and tradition, is something no designer accoutrement or fancy modernization can ever enhance, nor should it.

CLOCKWISE FROM TOP LEFT   *The sweet twin room features painted wooden floors; a mahogany four-poster bed in one of the villa's queen suites; Messel green trim on everything from the lounge's front doors to the shutters; cocktail hour in the open-air parlor.*

OPPOSITE PAGE   *Sunset reflected on the second-story wraparound terrace.*

FRENCHMAN'S LOOKOUT

TORTOLA, BRITISH VIRGIN ISLANDS

Atop one of the highest points on Tortola's West End, Frenchman's Lookout has one of the most magnificent, island-studded views in the entire Caribbean. Once you've earned your passage—climbing the steep driveway's 180-degree turn in second gear, the blue-trimmed 10,000-square-foot two-story Carolina-style house with double wraparound porches rewards you mightily with a truly commanding view of the Sir Francis Drake Channel, St. John, Little Thatch Island, and even Jost Van Dyke in the distance. The generous wooden decks of the porches are adorned with hammocks in every corner, various styles of seating arrangements, and on the ground level, a dining table to ensure as much time as possible can be spent indulging the view once favored by pirates. All of the five bedrooms, including their bathrooms, feature mahogany French double doors that open onto the verandas and are best left open to catch the omnipresent breeze that flows through the house. The fifty-foot, L-shaped pool lies alongside the house, facing the Channel and St. John, enjoying the same privileged view and constant breeze. Behind the pool sits a pale blue dining gazebo, a range grill and fridge, and a vibrant garden with pink bougainvillea, yellow frangipani, and a secluded hot tub overlooking the West End harbor and the small village of Soper's Hole. The flowing indoor-outdoor design and purposeful setup of Frenchman's Lookout are poised for the appreciation of its all-encompassing and sparkling visual asset. Lounging in one of the second-story hammocks (preferably the one to the southeast with its unencumbered view of a verdant island hump—Little Thatch—and the Channel's daily boat parade) is postcard-perfect Caribbean indulgence.

The property is managed by the amiable Lynn, who will greet you at the airport, transport you to the villa, peppering her tour with witty commentary and friendly suggestions and present you with your rental car. Upon entering the spacious house, you'll find the fruits of Lynn's planning and any of your own specific directions, plus a stocked fridge, toiletry-laden bathroom, and brimming basket of sunblocks and bug sprays. Lynn and the kind staff, including Gloria, the morning cook, make a point of assuring that no demand is too difficult, including arranging visits from the property's Indian spa therapists, Appu and Monali, who are nothing short of genius masseurs, to perform alfresco treatments on the porch. From the very first drop of hot oil to the well-placed elbow in your lower back to the cool tickle of sea breeze on your exposed skin, a complete catharsis is guaranteed. I repeat, do not miss this unforgettable treat.

The interior of the house plays second fiddle to the view but has a dignified and muted sophistication. Pale walls, terra-cotta tile floors, and decorative balustrades along the central staircase set an initial, carefree tone for the house. The spacious living room features two white couches, an elegant mahogany mirrored armoire, and cushioned rattan chairs that reflect the house's overall relaxed island style, while the dining room's long, polished banquet table, and brand-new gourmet kitchen point to the home's more updated, luxurious amenities. Frenchman's Lookout is so well-appointed, including having a separate gym building with billiards table and spacious yoga deck, that leaving the house can be quite trying. Luckily, the property's thirty-five-foot Contender yacht in the harbor down the hill makes a convincing case. Captain Simon, a dive master and marine naturalist, will happily ferry you on the comfortably cushioned boat to secluded neighboring islands (Money Bay, Norman Island, or Ginger Island) for superb snorkeling and to the beach bars like Foxy's to taste the special rum cocktails or enjoy a long lunch. Meals at Frenchman's tend to be self-arranged and thus simple and uncomplicated (Gloria can be kept on all day or private chefs may be brought in by prior arrangement), which is fitting, given that the views from all three different dining locations mesmerize the diner immediately. A memorable evening can easily be had by grilling locally-caught fish bought at the market down the hill and dining in the gazebo, with dessert being a view of the sunset from the six-person hot tub. An interesting bonus of the house is the strong AT&T cell signal, due to Frenchman's close proximity to St. John, U.S. Virgin Islands, so American cell-phone users luck out and won't have to pay roaming charges.

PREVIOUS PAGE   *One of the best nap locations in the Caribbean.*

OPPOSITE PAGE   *Light blue trim brightens the colonial-style architecture of Frenchman's Lookout.*

ABOVE   *Typical boat traffic sailing down the channel.*

ROOMS

The five bedrooms of Frenchman's Lookout are all elegantly and simply furnished with mahogany or iron four-poster beds, hotel-style white duvets, and billowing linen curtains on the sets of French doors. All of the rooms are upstairs except the first-floor bedroom, whose high ceilings, mahogany four-poster queen-size bed, and terra-cotta floors offer comfort and privacy from the other guests. The guest rooms upstairs include a master suite, a room with twin beds, a hotel-like tandem double-bed room, and a guest room with a king-size bed, plus an alcove office, complete with computer, high-speed Internet, printer, and fax, should work have to follow you down to the islands. The master suite is the clear top choice with the greatest number of French doors opening onto the deck and the southeast, which provides the room with front-row views of the pale sunrise and the bright moonlight. The room's lack of interior embellishments, save for a small sitting area with velveteen chaise longues and a treated oak armoire with flat-screen television, is welcome given the veranda's compelling tug outdoors. The master suite's spacious bathroom features a tiled walk-in shower, Jacuzzi tub, and two sets of French doors that open onto the deck so you can shower or bathe with a view. All of the rooms have air-conditioning though it's rarely used, since guests tend to prefer leaving the doors open to the trade winds and trusting the circulation to the room's ceiling fans. The most attractive room, however, is the room with double beds, which faces the southwest and features some of the more stylish furnishings, like handsome leather bed stools and a cracked leather sofa. The owner's hotel background is evident through the staid décor of the house and focus on quality linens (Frette), superior mattresses, and spacious bathrooms. Staying at Frenchman's Lookout will never be anything but supremely comfortable. According to Kate Moss (their unofficial celebrity spokesperson), it's her favorite spot in the Caribbean—and with good reason—Frenchman's Lookout is the ideal spot to convalesce and recharge.

OPPOSITE PAGE   *A view of the closest neighboring island—the U.S. Virgin island of St. John, from the dining room.*

CLOCKWISE FROM TOP LEFT   *The light-filled guest room makes waking up a treat; dried coral on display; French twin mahogany four-poster beds in a masculine-style guest room; polished traditionalism in the living room.*

FOLLOWING PAGE   *The otherworldly, island-dotted view.*

STEELE POINT

TORTOLA, BRITISH VIRGIN ISLANDS

*S*ituated on one of the most widely recognized points for mariners in the eastern Caribbean, the Steele Point villa, with its *Architectural Digest* pedigree and curious contemporary design, dangles over the rocky western edge of Tortola. The eight-acre private peninsula, known as Steele Point, could easily double as Tortola's social dispatch, given its front-row seat to the daily boat traffic between all the Virgin Islands. So intimate is the view that owner Irene Wilson and her children, Justin and Christine, claim they can deduce which island bar has the best crowd each day based on the characters they spy in the passing boats. Built by local architect Michael Helm entirely from cypress wood that was pulled out of Florida's Okeechobee swamp, the five-bedroom house sits perched on stilts and looks like a series of lifeguard stations, albeit far slicker. Set right into the rock, the modern-style villa is built in tiers on both sides of the point, so the 360-degree ocean views are so immediate and dramatic that the comparison of being on a boat is instantaneous—particularly from the extended deck that dangles off the end point. The cliffside pool, set closer to the villa's gravel entrance, stares directly at the edge of St. John and the daily procession of boats from Tortola's West End harbor. However, Steele Point's lush landscaping, lofty palms, cacti, blooming bougainvillea, and rocky coastline ensure substantial seclusion and privacy.

Given that the house is built into the rocky hillside, there are multiple levels, not to mention staircases, to contend with in order to get from room to room. The multi-level layout makes the villa feel more like a compound than a house.

The largest leveled area is where the main hub of the house lies. Surrounded by stone patios, one with a grill and seating area, and decks, the main structure features an open-air living area, dining room, guest bedroom, and gourmet kitchen. The boxlike architecture and glass walls keep the view on center stage while the decks bring a palpable intimacy with the water. Every detail in the custom-built villa was purposed and styled with modern flair. A careful selection of materials—wood, steel, limestone, and glass—keeps the house rooted in modernism while a collection of fine art and original sculpture helps soften and personalize the cool construction. The nerve center of the house, the newly remodelled kitchen, easily services the decks along with the interior dining room and cozy, elevated sitting area. Living right on the water, exposed to the sea's destructive salt air, the furniture of the villa must be as weatherproof as possible. The soft, natural-hued furnishings, wicker dining chairs, and exotic accents like copper Indonesian drum tables keep the interiors relaxed and absent of pretension. The "wow" factor is left to the sleek architecture, signature views, and enviable location. The experience at Steele Point is fashioned to be outdoors as much as possible. Guests traverse from one level to another (hopefully without fear of heights), choosing between various nooks to appreciate the omnipresent sunshine, breeze, and sea vistas. Sunsets are particularly spectacular at the villa given its western-facing point, and it's common to spot marine life like dolphins, sea turtles, rays, and even whales in the waters right off the house. Despite the villa's unspoiled, natural location it offers twenty-first-century luxury trimmings like Wi-Fi, satellite cable, and a U.S.-based cell signal from neighboring St. John. Steele Point also features an expansive dock area with space for two boats, which must be pre-arranged for usage, plus lounge chairs and a secluded sandy nook (ideal should the bathing suit feel optional) with ladders down into the sea for some surprisingly great snorkeling. There are two other, smaller villas on the peninsula that make up the entire Steele Point Estate. All three can be rented together, accommodating up to twenty-two people, but if five bedrooms are enough then the Steele Point villa's position at the very tip is the top choice.

ROOMS

With five bedrooms on four different levels, privacy is essentially guaranteed. The studio room sits tucked up behind the main building, totally on its own, facing north towards Jost van Dyke on the "rougher" Atlantic Ocean side. The site of the previous owner's painting studio, the room has been entirely refurbished with a queen-size bed, sleek bathroom fixtures, and floor-to-ceiling glass walls looking out at the view.

PREVIOUS PAGES   *The architectural feat of Steele Point Villa.*

ABOVE, FROM LEFT   *The sleek lines of Steele Point's design; the rustic, chic interior in the double guest room.*

BELOW   *A more contemporary bathroom in the artist's studio suite.*

OPPOSITE PAGE   *The dangling construction and its eye-popping views.*

There's also a small porch with nylon-and-steel deck chairs that may incite vertigo in some and in others a total tropical fantasy, as it truly feels like a deck on the edge of the world. Perfect for honeymooners (or a couple) an outdoor shower, a small kitchenette with granite counters and minfridge, and a constant soundtrack of crashing waves complete this charming retreat. The rest of the rooms are divided between one just off the main building by the living room and the rest in another separate structure with three levels that descend the rock face down to the dock and sea. The master bedroom is located on the second level down. With views of Little Thatch Island and its deserted beach plus a spacious porch with two chaise longues to soak up the daytime sun and view the passing boats, it's the easiest room from which to appreciate the finest assets of Steele Point's remarkable location. The embroidered linens on the king-size bed and bronze sculptures in the room add a personalized touch to this otherwise plainly styled space. The faded gray color of the wood-plank walls and brushed limestone floors once again ensure that the eye travels outdoors without distraction. The final two rooms are on the lowest level and located just a few feet from the sea, and include private stone terraces, balconies, and separate bathroom suites with outdoor pebble-lined showers. All of the rooms have air-conditioning, but at Steele Point, leaving your doors open to the breeze and sounds of the sea is the whole idea.

OPPOSITE PAGE *Marble meets wooden planks in Steele Point's contemporary interiors.*

ABOVE *The villa's warm entrance and cliffside pool just below.*

GUANA ISLAND

PRIVATE ISLAND, BRITISH VIRGIN ISLANDS

The eighth-largest island in the chain of British Virgin Islands and just north of Tortola, Guana is named after its iguana-shaped rock outcrop on the northwestern coast. As one of the few remaining private islands in the world, Guana is a true island hideaway where seclusion and distance from the throngs of tourists are sincere guarantees. The verdant 850-acre island sanctuary features seven pristine, sandy beaches and miles of tropical orchards, marsh ponds, rocky mountains, grassy valleys, and even bat caves. Similar to its island neighbors, Guana was inhabited before Columbus's explorations, by the Arawakan-speaking Taíno Indians, and then the Caribs (where the word *Caribbean* comes from). Next came the Dutch and then the British in 1672. In the eighteenth century, two Quaker families, the Lakes and the Parkes, lived on the island and grew cotton and sugarcane. When the Quakers left, the island reverted to local ownership: the Frett and Shirley families from Tortola. In 1935 a couple from Massachusetts bought the island and began to build a few cottages on it, attracting outsiders to visit. In 1975, the current owners, Henry and Gloria Jarecki of New York, bought the island and have since restored the original Spartan cottages, constructed a modern owner's cottage, and invested in the island's land conservation and wildlife population, deeming the island a nature preserve and wildlife sanctuary. Under the Jareckis' stewardship, many plant forms and species have been reintroduced to the island, including the roseate flamingo, the Anegada iguana, the red-legged tortoise, and the white-crowned pigeon. The animals and flora flourish on Guana due to the undisturbed nature of the island—there's no marina, airport, or public facilities of any kind, well, other than the fruit and vegetable orchard, a whitewashed beach stand, and miles of marked hiking trails. The average number of guests on the island at any time is thirty, so humans also barely make a dent. With one coast on the calm Caribbean Sea and the other along the windier, immense Atlantic Ocean, Guana offers a wonderful diversity of vistas. To walk around the entire island takes at least eight hours, depending on your pace, though there are twenty-six other well-marked, shorter hikes that are guaranteed to provide the sort of awe-inspiring scenic points you'd imagine. Be sure to pack hiking shoes or sneakers with good treads as sometimes the trails can get steep. The hike to Bigelow Beach is one of the more challenging hikes but you are highly rewarded along the way with the view from the tallest point of the island and at the end, one of the most remote beaches in all of the Caribbean—plus the staff will leave a picnic lunch for you and then ferry you back by boat if desired.

The nature-oriented focus of Guana allows guests to instantly let their hair down and appreciate their surroundings in a totally different way than at more buttoned-up resorts. Arriving at the island via boat-transfer from Tortola's airport is an excellent precursor to the entire Guana experience. The somewhat choppy ride is soothed by the initial sight of White Bay Beach's powder-white sand, perfect crescent shape, and absence of umbrellas, chairs, and—best of all—people. After you pull up to the small dock, the affable manager Jason heartily shakes your hand, ushering you into his manager's golf cart and assuring you that your luggage will get to the right place while he gives you the lay of the land. For an island of 850 acres, the tour is surprisingly quick, as the paved roads make just one ring in the center of the island. First there's the postcard-perfect beach with its small wooden bar and changing area, followed by two sandy tennis courts begging for play, and a small wooden sign that points the way down a leafy path to the humble, beachside canvas pavilion and deck, otherwise known as the spa. It's evident that Guana is not about five-star luxury amenities but rather the unpolluted views (including that of the night stars, which they tout upon arrival) and access to a truly unspoiled landscape. Their tagline—"the Virgin Island that still is"—is reassuringly accurate.

The daily schedule at Guana is surprisingly routine, though, of course, all of it can be adapted to guests' individual desires upon request. Breakfast, lunch, tea, cocktails, and dinner are all served from set hours in the hilltop main house, known as Dominica. While the menu is rather limited comparable to other resorts (choices range from the beef or the fish) the food is always fresh. Dinner may include pan-fried grouper with sweet-

potato puree and cauliflower *au gratin* followed by passion fruit sorbet and pineapple tart. The dining area's simple, whitewashed stone building recalls Greek island architecture, complete with a blue door and shutters, and features a small honesty bar area, library, and casual lounge. The dining tables are scattered out on the covered verandas on either side of the building plus a few romantic options along the cliff edge. The Atlantic-facing side has far more tables and space, so choosing to have breakfast or the buffet lunch facing the Caribbean sea and White Bay Beach will feel more private. This island property is nothing if not creative with its social offerings,

including Full-Moon Parties and Old Movie Nights shown after dinner in the garden pavilion area (which also hosts yoga classes on request) located just behind the main house. A perfect spot for families, particularly with curious and active children, Guana's well-tended orchard not only features countless varieties of fruit trees and plants, but also a pair of sweet-natured donkeys. Plus there's a small museum that highlights the island's history and wildlife and showcases a few artifacts that have been found on the island. Resident scientist and head gardener, Dr. Liao, who has been on island for twenty-three years, will happily speak with guests about his

research, species rehabilitation, and reintroduction program and care over the orchard. For bird watchers, Guana's fifty different species are a surefire delight while nature enthusiasts will indulge in the trails and fourteen different reptile species (all harmless). Given Guana's strong allegiance to protecting the natural landscape and wildlife mixed with the laid-back atmosphere and minimal building construction (there's no shared pool on the island), the island offers a unique alternative to the staid, glossy Caribbean experience. If it's the natural Caribbean landscape that you're after, there's no better spot to find it than Guana.

ROOMS

The accommodations on the island range from one-bedroom stone guest cottages, including the ultra-private North Cottage on its own Atlantic beach on the northern coast, to more modern, two- to three-bedroom villas and the stately owner's villa, Jost House. There are no televisions or phones in the stone cottage rooms (though there is Wi-Fi) and the furnishings are purposely kept minimal. Ceiling fans keep the rooms cool during the day while low-slung beds, albeit king-sized, and simple white desks and dressers complete the room. The spacious, adobe-style bathrooms with outdoor showers distinguish the cottages (all named after Caribbean islands) with a touch of forethought luxury. Given the cottage's hilltop location, the trade winds, fierce in the winter months, can be heard blowing right through the cottage's wood-frame roofs and even rattling the wooden doors and shutters during the winds' heights. The effect is somewhat eerie yet undeniably atmospheric, and waking up to that sparkling view quells any residual discomfort. Welcome packets containing a pen flashlight, hat, waterproof fanny pack, trail maps, and other goodies are stocked in the rooms so that guests are outfitted in Guana-wear and guaranteed souvenirs right off the bat. (There's also a simple gift shop should there be a hankering for even more color options.) Each of the rooms has minibars that come stocked with its guest's preference of beverages, gleaned prior to arrival, along with generous cans

of bug spray (a noted inevitability of staying on an island nature preserve). The rustic, laid-back character of Guana is a source of pride and statements of how "nothing has changed" since the late '70s certainly feel accurate when sitting inside the cottages or Dominca's corner library and worn living room. The addition of the more modern Jost House poses a direct contrast to the hillside cottages and should be reserved for those unable to be without television, marble bathrooms, indoor dining rooms, and a pool. Otherwise, the simple white cottages appear to be the most direct route to absorbing the true nature of the Guana experience. The three multi-bedroom villas are also considerably up-to-date in comparison to the cottages; some even boast a pool, though far less decadent than the Jost House. The villa interiors are festooned with colorful murals of tropical scenes and bright hues of yellows, oranges and pinks are abundant. Nevertheless, I prefer the modest all-white cottages, not only for their simplicity but for their proximity to the main house, making activities such as the beach, meals, and movie nights more readily accessible. The lack of buildings on the island mean that nighttime on Guana is very dark. It's no wonder flashlights are given to each guest upon arrival—they are necessary tools to navigate back to your room after dinner. Of course, the flipside is that the stars on Guana are wonderfully clear, seemingly close enough to touch. My other favorite accommodation option on Guana is the

secluded North Cottage. So remote and cut-off from the rest of the island, clothing for its guests becomes optional. Situated right on the beach with its own dock and golf cart (necessary for evening transport), the North Cottage defines "beach hideaway." Though far less appointed than Jost House, the North Cottage presents the rustic beach style reminiscent of houses designed thirty to forty years ago. Louvered windows frame larger glassed-in windows while exposed beams fill the gabled ceilings, giving the cottage a bungalow feel, with dark wooden walls, raffia carpets, and simple wicker and slip-covered furnishings. The expansive terrace beckons with lounge chairs and a small pool and leads out onto a small dock, which easily claims the best spot for stargazing on the island. The rougher Atlantic sea provides the ideal soundtrack. For utter privacy and communing with island nature, there's no better spot in the Caribbean (short of pitching a tent on a remote beach) than North Cottage on Guana. The island is also available for full buy-outs where a maximum of thirty-two guests can share the island and have all the secluded privileges to themselves. The other tagline of Guana's marketing pitch is "imagine the Caribbean before it went public" and though slogans usually tend to sensationalize their offerings, once again this remark rings true; Guana island may very well be the closest thing there is to going back in time, island style.

OPPOSITE PAGE   *Guana's über-private, white sandy beach.*

ABOVE, CLOCKWISE FROM TOP LEFT   *An adobe-style shower; minimal décor in the whitewashed
guest rooms; informal signage mark's the availability of Guana's spa; the Greek–inspired blue doors.*

AQUAMARE

VIRGIN GORDA, BRITISH VIRGIN ISLANDS

Conceived with the notion of creating rental villas that look and feel like high-end hotel suites, each of Aquamare's three identical, five-bedroom beachfront villas feature gleaming, name-brand fixtures, polished marble floors, and tucked-in bed-corners that signal the presence of high-minded luxury. Built in 2008 and co-owned by four friends from Puerto Rico, the villas are a composite of each of their dream vacation homes mixed with totems of their favorite hotels. Overlooking Virgin Gorda's serene Mahoe Bay, the three 8,000-square-foot island-style villas are set back from the private half-mile-long beach, arranged in an isosceles triangle, affording each villa unobstructed views of the multihued water and distant boat traffic on Sir Francis Drake Channel. The exquisite, wood-framed villas are a welcome update to the traditional island style, using not one but five different woods, including Brazilian ipe on the decks and Spanish cedar in the vaulted ceilings, yet maintaining the classic shingled roof and indoor-outdoor layout. Architect Liselott Johnsson designed the profile of the roofs to resemble barnacles and reflect the surrounding mountains. All three villas can be rented together and make an especially decadent, not to mention effortless, backdrop given Aquamare's list of pre-set service providers, to any major celebration. The beach is even equipped with electricity! Listening to co-owner Guillermo Paz describe his birthday dinner on the beach, complete with bonfire, produces enough party-envy to want to invent a reason to celebrate at Aquamare.

Although the villas are often rented out separately, their close proximity, about thirty to forty yards from one another, makes it far more comfortable when shared among friends and family. Given the villas' identical structure and luxurious appointments—each one including a spacious, vaulted living room, gourmet kitchen, indoor and outdoor lounge and dining areas, infinity pool, three master suites, and two premium suites—choosing among the three becomes about the location. While all three villas are surrounded by lush tropical gardens (sometimes too lush, inviting hordes of mosquitoes) and feel equally private, only one truly fronts the beach, allowing the sound of lapping waves to filter into the guest rooms at night.

The villas' hotel-style inspiration pervades the smooth, neutral-toned interiors and sleek textiles. Twill-covered couches, cushy beige armchairs, and John Robshaw pillows keep the living rooms' style streamlined and smart while tripod floor lamps and teak deck chairs with navy piping add a bit of texture. The natural palette and high ceilings create an overall soothing and confident effect (having followed architecture's golden rule of proportions). Each villa's fully equipped, professional-grade kitchen comes stocked with your pre-ordered selections and elegant Rosenthal china. The double refrigerator, wine fridge, and ice maker will make you forget your remote island surroundings while the range oven and ample counter space will appease any chef, including the roster of private chefs the villas' concierge has on hand. Aquamare's sophistication (and cleanliness) seems wholly different from other Caribbean island villas—as if transplanted from California. The villas' services, modeled again after high-end hotels, include an on-site concierge who will coordinate everything from meals on the beach to rental cars, dinner reservations, and spa services. Aquamare also boasts its own sixty-two-foot power yacht and a thirty-six-foot Tiara cruising yacht, which can be rented for an extra charge, and is well worth it. The sixty-two-foot Azimut, *Motivation*, is yet another emblem of Aquamare's opulence and so worth the extra expenditure. Cruising around the island's crystal-clear waters, stopping at secluded beaches and secret snorkeling spots, then enjoying a light lunch or drinks while on board the boat's comfortable, cushioned design provides one of those vacation memories (of decadence) that you'll recall long after the sunburn has faded. Not to be outdone by its own marine offerings, Aquamare even has its own line of signature spa treatments that are administered on site. Once you've picked your setting (beach, terrace, or even the guest rooms' sizable outdoor showers) the options range from deep tissue to hot-stone massages to island-inspired body wraps. Beyond the luxury trimmings and fancy toys, Aquamare's most prized privilege is its exceptional, secluded location on the quiet, western coast of the island. Brand new

PREVIOUS PAGE   *The beachfront Villa Number 1 of Aquamare's trio of luxe accommodations.*

OPPOSITE PAGE   *The guestroom's deck and hammock—romantic at any time of day or night.*

ABOVE   *No shortage of plush seating in the villa's living rooms at Aquamare.*

kayaks and a basket of snorkel sets are left on the beach for a reason—the snorkeling right in front is remarkably colorful, while paddling to neighboring Savannah Bay—voted one of the prettiest beaches in the Caribbean—is a daily must. For lounging, the beach's signature swinging daybed and cushioned lounge chairs invite zero criticism—only long-lasting memories of utter relaxation. One of Aquamare's less touted attributes is its sunset view—best appreciated from the daybed. I know I'll never forget lying on my stomach and watching the horizon line grow sharper as the setting sun sent its kaleidoscopic colors into the sky.

ROOMS

The five bedrooms in each of Aquamare's three villas are equally well-appointed. The three master suites are stacked one on top of one another in a tower, each with private terraces complete with dangling hammocks, lounge chairs, and sea views. Just like the preferred hotel-suites of the owners, Aquamare's rooms are amenity filled with 400-thread-count Frette linens, a pillow menu for the king-size beds, Bulgari toiletries, minifridges, and flat-screen televisions with satellite cable and DVD players. While some may find the luxury markings a tad sterile for the Caribbean, few can complain about the brand-new mattresses and daily housekeeping, which includes turn-down service. Similar to the living room décor, the master suites have pale color schemes with John Robshaw headboards and minimal, muted furnishings like tasseled chaises, plantation-style bed benches, and decorative porcelain drums used as side tables. The high point of each guest room, though, is the massive bathroom with double vanities, central Jacuzzi tub, and perhaps one of the most lavishly

designed outdoor shower. Enclosed in dark latticed wood or stone walls and shaded by the surrounding palms and ginger flowers, each spacious shower has room enough for five with a powerful central rain shower that streams like a waterfall. Showering becomes a sensual experience no matter the intent. Each villa's other two rooms are on the other side of the main pavilion and were originally designed for traveling nannies or children, featuring twin beds and both indoor and outdoor showers. Defiantly different than most hideaways, the rooms at Aquamare are set up to compete with the view and natural surroundings—and to encourage equal pleasure and comfort. Their exposure to the outdoors, albeit manicured, feels intimate when you leave the terrace doors open to the breeze or float in the hammock. And at night you can sleep soundly, assured of the fancy hotel experience you've come to cherish and expect.

FROM LEFT *The spacious bathrooms with soak tubs and outdoor rain showers;*
pressed linens and John Robshaw headboards ensure a good night sleep.

Double vanities, marble countertops, and Bulgari bath products—similar to a five-star hotel.

PENINSULA HOUSE

LAS TERRENAS, DOMINICAN REPUBLIC

*L*ike a vision in white, the Victorian-style Peninsula House appears, ethereal, on a hilltop clearing amid towering palm trees and the flowering, sultry jungle. Whether it's the bumpy final hour of the three-hour drive from Santo Domingo or, more likely, the utter contrast to the area's humble surroundings that the house's ornate gingerbread trim poses, the first glimpse of the pale

clapboard exterior and wraparound verandas is almost absurdly gratifying. Twenty minutes from the surf town of Las Terrenas, on the southern coast of the breathtaking Samaná Peninsula in the Dominican Republic, the six-bedroom guest house perched high on the hill above Coson Beach claiming an ocean-filled panorama has quickly become a destination. Its sheer singularity mixed with elegantly formal design and an exquisitely detailed approach has granted the newly constructed property (2008) some considerable recognition. Fortunately, its remote location and small size cement its hideaway nature.

Stepping onto the front porch of the property and standing under the classic portico entry with views all the way through the brick patio courtyard into the peach-colored living room and out past the opposing veranda to the glittering ocean is like peering through C.S. Lewis' infamous wardrobe. The multitude of decorative details and artful touches, even at first sight—from the mirrored window arches to the Victorian-style column trim to the tall Moroccan floor lanterns and framed oil paintings on the back walls—will make your eyes dance about. I had to keep myself from tearing through the house, eager to see more.

Peninsula House's marked sophistication, including its custom eighteeth-

century inspired design, is credited to its French owner, Marie-Claude Thiebault. After living in Provence for many years, she and her partner, the charming and talented chef Cary Guy, decided to head to the Caribbean to try their hand at running a small inn. Once the appropriate site was found (much to their surprise) in the Dominican Republic, Marie-Claude and Cary packed up the house in Provence, filling fourteen containers with valuables such as seventeenth-century furnishings and priceless objets d'art. During the construction of the main house, a true labor of love, Marie-Claude and Cary lived in the adjacent pool pavilion, knowing their on-property vigilance would ensure their vision would be completed correctly. As expected, the construction was not without its delays and characteristic Caribbean pitfalls, but in the end, the estate turned out just as they had intended: a replica of an eighteenth-century Caribbean plantation house with Victorian trimmings.

The manse, as it now stands, is 18,000 square feet of clapboard, carved window treatments, sweeping verandas, and French doors, and is an undeniable achievement—particularly within its surrounding environment. To be a guest at the Peninsula House is to witness the art of genuine hospitality—attentive, unob-

trusive service in a superior, finely appointed environ. Both owners, along with Marie-Claude's charming son, Thomas Stamm, are always available to guests, particularly at mealtime when they take turns waiting; yet through subtle behavior they also set a distinguished tone of separation, truly inviting the guest to treat the house as his or her own. And what a treat that is, with refined interiors featuring a Louis XVI silk settee, works by Seruchi Chang, one of India's top painters from Bombay; eighteenth-century Burmese and Indonesian marionette puppets; an ancient Chinese artifact dating from BC; and drawings by famous Greek artist Alekos Fassianos illustrating poems of French poet Paul Seghers. And if a rarefied elegance, particularly in the Caribbean, wasn't noted instantly upon entry, then the total of twenty-one antique crystal chandeliers hanging throughout the property (including at least one in each suite) are distinct hints at the property's illustrious décor. Even though the sofas are covered with J. H. Thorpe *tissage* fabric in the drawing room and the library, the French doors out to the veranda are forever open, allowing the elements to freely mix with the delicate interiors of the house. The veranda's wicker seating area pairs elegant Turkish carpets underneath, alerting the guests to the house's distinct refned and relaxed atmosphere. The adjacent billiard room is the most popular spot in the house.

The grounds at Peninsula House are beautifully manicured, with a brick-lined pool and teak loungers scattered underneath the yard's stage-set curved palms. The house's beach club is a five-minute ride down the hill and features a popular restaurant and casual bar with changing rooms, loungers, and towels for the customary pre- and post-lunch dip. (The restaurant's chocolate ice cream is fast becoming a local favorite.) Meals back at the house, however, are an exquisite highlight, prepared by Cary (a French-trained chef) and served either on the veranda or in the courtyard which, when candlelit, is otherworldly and a must for romantics. Dishes like shrimp in passion fruit sauce, grilled langoustine with mango butter, and gazpacho with mustard ice cream are presented on Limoge china with New World and European wines decanted and poured into crystal glasses. The vintage napkin rings, a favorite collectible of Marie-Claude, are obscure finds from her travels abroad and in France. At breakfast, three different juices are presented in crystal carafes and the fruit spreads are housed in antique silver sets. Nothing has been put away or saved for a special occasion: the finest china, crystal, and silverware are used for each and every guest just as delicate napkin linens are ironed and fresh each day. The presentation is nothing short of stunning, while the impressive quality make the guest feel appreciated and moreover, delightfully privileged. The house's symmetrical layout (almost Italianate inside) and inner courtyard flanked by two staircases give it a grand tone. The open-air hallway on the second floor with nothing but six large bedroom doors and a small library area in the landing over the front portico means guests, and the owners, can easily note one another's movements—especially since the heavy doors can sometimes slam from the wind.

Though rest assured, the delicious freedom from an organized schedule (mealtimes are more or less up to you) means no one is paying attention.

ROOMS

The six guest rooms, each averaging 550 square feet, claim no fancy names or cheeky monikers. Rather, they bear simple numbers, permitting the interiors to speak for themselves. Like the first floor, the individually designed rooms benefit from the exquisite furnishings and international and historic collectibles of Marie-Claude. Spied from the second floor's wraparound balcony, the identical sets of French doors give no indication to the wonder that lie inside. Room number 5, my top choice, is one of the two back-facing rooms with direct views of the property's rolling, palm-studded lawn, black-bottomed pool, and chapel gazebo. High ceilings, two sets of French doors, and ceiling fans keep the air circulating throughout the room (sometimes creating wind tunnels). Air-conditioning at night, though, is recommended, given the absence of mosquito netting and screens. The room's long, rectangular shape allows for a separate sitting area with an antique French settee done in yellow silk, locally made mahogany coffee table, and a stately wooden desk that is actually a nineteenth-century English dining server found by Marie-Claude in South Africa. The hardwood floors and polished, dark, tatajuba-framed four-poster bed are softened by small Turkish rugs. The mahogany-lined bathroom

features fresh ginger flowers cut daily by Marie-Claude herself, sensual olive-oil soaps and shampoos, and framed engravings of seventeenth-century Europe. A delightful sophistication surrounds the room, no doubt gleaned from the elegant furnishings and global accents, such as nineteenth-century Indonesian puppets and framed prints from a Tibetan prayer book. As a result, the room intrigues as much as it awes the guest. The other five rooms are equally stunning featuring similar high ceilings, crown moldings and Frette linens, though they do vary in styles of furnishing and layout. Each room comes equipped with flat-screen televisions with satellite programming, DVDs, and Bose docking stations for iPods. If you forget your iPod, not to worry, Peninsula House has extras fully loaded with music. The house also boasts a strong wireless signal making the necessary quick email allowable from the second story veranda's seating area. One of the hotel's two front bedrooms, number 2, is another favorite with cool gray walls and a Victorian-inspired marble bathroom. If possible, request a tour from Marie-Claude of any of the other rooms should they be available. To hear her detail the interiors and narrate the origins of each furnishing is to gain an even larger appreciation, if at all possible, for the irrefutable excellence of Peninsula House.

CLOCKWISE FROM TOP LEFT   *The brick-lined, black-bottomed pool; one of Marie-Claude's many antique finds; another precious artifact collected from travels in the Orient; an ornate guest room with precious, antique seating and mahogany four-poster beds.*

OPPOSITE PAGE   *Artifacts and signature collectibles decorate the parlor room of the truly unique Dominican property.*

OPPOSITE PAGE *The romantic inner courtyard can be reserved for private meals.*

ABOVE, CLOCKWISE FROM TOP LEFT *The al-fresco sitting room; an antique canopy bed found in Provence; an antique, silk-embroidered French bergère wingback chair in a guestroom; pewter-colored walls keep this oft-requested guestroom nice and cool.*

LALUNA

GRENADA

*T*he continued success of LaLuna, the heralded decade-old boutique hotel and forefather of boutique properties in the Caribbean (according to Italian owner Bernardo Bertucci) is evident upon arrival. In typical hideaway fashion, the road to the property winds away from towns, past busy beaches, and grows increasingly rough as it approaches the secluded slice of paradise.

After waving to the dozing guard, whose narrow white house is every bit the terrific prop, drink in the hotel's sixteen rustic-chic cottages, complete with thatched roofs and bright, Old World Italian-style paint jobs, and the phenomenally picturesque white, sandy beach and crystal-clear cerulean water. The combination of a drop-dead gorgeous location and the influence of the Italian pace of life, LaLuna was beyond well positioned for acclaim. Opened at the end of 2000 by Bernardo, a former fashion-marketing exec (Prada, Armani, La Perla), LaLuna has been the toast of every glossy magazine since its inception and continues to collect rave reviews with its recent expansion, which includes a beachfront yoga pavilion and Balinese-style spa. Nevertheless, the hotel maintains its off-the-beaten-track character by refusing to expand the accommodation offerings, instead focusing on improving the types of amenities and the quality of the dining in an effort to appease its hard-to-impress clientele.

Bernardo's background in fashion and design has manifested itself in LaLuna's consistent and heavy reliance upon a set style motto. At LaLuna, the style is overwhelmingly Balinese. After living in Bali for two years, Bernardo developed an ardent passion for all things Balinese. Almost every piece of furniture on the property was imported from Bali—even the therapists in the spa are Balinese. What's worth noting is that Bernardo's fondness for Balinese furniture and his importation of it to the Caribbean was founded well before the current craze and is yet another element behind LaLuna's storied appeal. Despite the somewhat strict adherence to one particular style, the carved teak daybed, plantation-style chairs, and cushioned platform benches of the poolside lounge are no less inviting. Thatch-style roofs and natural pigment–colored cottages (using water-based paint from Italy) with stained deck flooring and authentic Indonesian goddess woodcarvings complete the regimented motif that surprisingly does not travel into the hotel's signature restaurant. Definitively Italian, the open-air, beachside restaurant serves typical Mediterranean-style Italian cuisine, such as *insalata di polpo*, or octopus salad, for lunch, although a pizza or simple pasta dish makes for the more reliable meal selection. Dinner is a more prodigious affair, drawing an outside crowd that has heard about the Italian chef Daniele's charcuterie, which includes prosciutto and bresaola flown in monthly from Italy, and authentic entrées like osso bucco and homemade papardelle.

The restaurant also offers some worthwhile Italian wines (a rarity in the Caribbean), ensuring the entire meal is as close to Italy as you will ever find in Grenada. As expected, the coffee served at the restaurant is not only delicious and strong, but also available at any hour. The property's spa (opened December 2008) and massive yoga pavilion overlooking the beach have transformed the property into a spa destination offering three different yoga styles and a range of Asian-inspired treatments. Still in its early stages—the treatment rooms could stand more insulation as the thin, reedlike walls don't quite muffle your neighbor's sighs of contentment and the locker rooms have only one shower each—the spa will surely undergo further enhancements after this writing. But regardless of future plans for the spa, its initial existence has already given Bernardo just what he needed: a new outlet for his Balinese fascination. The property's alluring, private beach is decorated with elephant-grass umbrellas and offers excellent swimming and enough space to spread out away from other guests. If yoga is not in session, then the chairs and the elevated, flat patch of sand in front of the pavilion present the most tranquil sunbathing spot. Kayaks and Hobie Cats are available for guests; LaLuna's secluded location offers excellent sightseeing from the water of Grenada's volcanic coastline.

LaLuna is very much a personal spot—Bernardo's baby that he's constantly nurturing and adjusting based on feedback and new ideas (his first child is actually named Luna). Every detail, including the Louis Armstrong music

playing in the lounge and the white pizzette (minipizzas) that are passed intermittently between lunch and dinner, must first pass muster with Bernardo. He is the indispensable force behind LaLuna and it is his charming and enthusiastic demeanor, particularly with his guests, that keeps his reservations full and his reviews positive. Of course, the innate Italian sensibility (good food = happy people) doesn't hurt, either.

ROOMS

As Bernardo recounts the story of working with an atypical architect to design the place, he is amazed at just how little has changed from the original drawings, despite over ten years passing. The entire layout of the property was based upon the architect's intent to communicate a feeling of relaxation. The sixteen free-standing cottages lie staggered evenly on the hill, a few right down on the beach, and all have individual plunge pools and spacious front porches. Each cottage features gauzy, billowing curtains tied to the wooden poles of the porch which, when drawn, signal a most definitive do-not-disturb sign to the staff. The one-bedroom cottages are simply if not sparsely furnished with four-poster queen-size beds and cushioned benches along the wall, perfect for draping clothes. The televisions have satellite cable channels and DVD players, plus the minibar comes fully stocked, complete with ground Illy brand coffee and French-press cafetiéres, easily allowing for the cottages to become self-sufficient havens for a few hours, if not the whole day. The adjoining open-air

bathrooms feature outdoor showers that are exposed to the interior of the bathroom, though the toilets are encased in separate closets. The configuration is a bit odd, given that outdoor showers are usually constructed for their view; this one faces inside and rather than close in the whole area that requires light, a sure-fire mosquito magnet at night, only the toilet is protected. Cottage 5 is halfway up the hill, slightly tucked away within surrounding trees and bushes but still has nice views. The polished stone floors of the room keep it nice and cool (as does the air-conditioning and ceiling fan) while the orange hand-painted walls give the room a comforting glow. French doors lead out from the bed onto the porch; their thick muslin curtains can easily be left open at night, though I would recommend that only for those close enough to the hear the lull of the waves. Due to the cottages' hillside locations, some require more of a upward hike than others. Before booking it's wise to ask just how many steps are involved from the beach to your front porch. For the ultimate in privacy, I recommend the cottages in the middle rows on either far end of the hill—preferably the side farthest from the restaurant to minimize the chance of hearing others, or of being overheard. Luckily, guests at LaLuna aren't the type to raise a ruckus and all seem similarly aligned to appreciating the architect's intent. A blissful week or long weekend at LaLuna (Air Jamaica flies directly to Grenada) answers your body's (and wandering mind's) pleas for that fantastical tropical getaway—pina colada and serene beach included.

CLOCKWISE FROM TOP LEFT *Indonesian carvings alongside LaLuna's simple logo; bright yellow walls cheer up a guest room; linen curtains offer a billowing separation between the bedroom and the porch; the indoor–outdoor design of the bathrooms.*

The owner's fanatical admiration for Balinese design is evident in the outdoor lounge area.

BEL AIR PLANTATION

GRENADA

The thirty-minute drive from Grenada's airport to the ginger-bread cottages of Bel Air Plantation is marked by the dramatic swing in Grenadian scenery. Ranging from a two-lane highway complete with billboards and glass office buildings to narrow, country roads that climb through thick tropical foliage past squat, tin houses, the drive serves as its own mini-pictorial guide to the

transition from urban angst to remote, island lifestyle. The hideaway's turnoff from the main road is appropriately tricky to find. The property's small sign is easily lost in the palm-filled brush, so instead look for the few tall masts peeking out from the neighboring shipyard and small harbor of St. David's. The long gravel driveway leads down toward the end of the small point (the location of Grenada's first European settlement by the French) with the quiet bay on the right and the shoulder of a lush hillside on the left. And with nary a neighbor, save for the quiet shipyard and small office cottage, the arrival to Bel Air Plantation is laced with tingling suspense.

A few hundred yards beyond the shipyard, two brightly painted cottages connected by an overhead periwinkle-and-pink-painted walkway can be seen, flanking the palm-fringed road like gate-houses to Candyland. The colorful entrance sets the tone for the carefree, cheerful oasis catering to those coming from land and sea. Tucked in the less-populated southeastern side of the island, Bel Air Plantation is every bit the secluded island escape that those stuck in an office find themselves fantasizing about. The property's eighteen acres of lush waterfront hillside and tropical gar-

dens provide ideal island imagery while the eleven latticed cottages, each painted a bold combination of candy-colored tones, perfect the dramatic fantasy. The gatehouses are actually the hotel's office and reception areas as well as the communal market that caters to both guests in the cottages and on visiting boats. Although the name Bel Air Plantation conjures up a land-based focus, this seaside property is all about the water. (To be fair, the name actually comes from owner Susan Fisher's maternal family's sugar plantation in Guyana). Originally from New Jersey, Susan, along with her husband, Fred, an accomplished classic shipwright whose studio is adjacent to the shipyard, set the deliberate laid-back tone of the Plantation by being an approachable fixture at the hotel's waterside restaurant, lounge, and bar area. Decorated in what can only be described as an informal yacht-club style with light wooden walls, model boats, and modest black-and-white sailboat prints, the two-story building, complete with wrap-around decking on both floors, is the central hub of the property and meeting point for land and sea guests alike. The upstairs lounge is filled with wicker sofas and sets of chairs around chess tables, making it the ideal location to congregate for games and a more sedate spot to

enjoy a cocktail. The downstairs features terrace dining and a gazebo-style bar with cushioned stools that swivel out toward the bay, to the delight of their sometimes rum-indulged occupants. Meals are taken at either the Barlow Tyrie teak tables on the terrace or on the stone patio. Candlelight and white table-cloths dress the tables up at night while bright blue napkins and cushions keep it relaxed and charming during the day. The overall mood is incredibly relaxed and cheerful, though of course this can be affected by the varying guests on any given night. During the regatta weekend the bar is filled with a particularly wonderful cast of characters, including Susan's childhood friend Janice, who performs with her band at the regatta's final-night party.

There is a stone and dirt path that starts just across from the restaurant and runs up through the hibiscus-filled gardens past a few of the lower-slung cottages and the pool, creating a summer camp feel. The infinity edge pool with a stone terrace hangs out from the hill and is just large enough to fit every guest, though it is far better when occupied by only a few. From the pool, the view of the bay and its bobbing boats is center stage while the surrounding gardens supply a palette of vibrant pinks and reds. The pool furniture is hardly fancy, reinforcing the informality of the property. The nearby pool house has two bathrooms, a stack of fresh towels, and a phone for drinks service, making it a compelling all-day location. Guests are left to their own whims with full kitchenettes in their cottages and minimal, do-it-yourself-style amenities like

PREVIOUS PAGE *Bel Air's small but sufficient pool bar area.*

OPPOSITE PAGE *One the resort's candy-colored gingerbread cottages.*

BELOW, FROM TOP TO BOTTOM *Sunset views right from bed; the picturesque harbor at dusk.*

kayaks. The hotel is a convivial refuge, appealing to both those who seek seclusion and serenity beyond the cruise ships of Grenada's main port and sailors who have come to the largest island in the Grenadines on the final leg of their trip, looking to round out the final, lazy days of their Caribbean vacation.

ROOMS

The eleven gingerbread-style cottages vary in size (studios, and one- and two-bedrooms), though all feature a generous front porch complete with brightly painted rocking chairs and Adirondack chairs angled to soak up the view over St. David's Bay. Built directly into the hill at varying heights (some are on stilts to maximize the panorama), each cottage is guaranteed privacy. Given the staggered layout, some houses get a wider, less tree-obstructed view while others feel a bit more removed from the crowd and action due to their high-tiered position. It's best to speak with Susan when booking as she can recommend which one is best suited to your taste and priorities. Each of the cottages feature furnishings that Susan finds during her annual trip to High Point Market in North Carolina as well as fabrics she sourced from Hawaii and California to give the interiors a purposefully tropical character. As Susan describes it, Bel Air Plantation was her opportunity to create something casual but eclectic and most importantly, authentically Caribbean. Scattered around the property and in various cottages are paintings by local artist Susan

Mains and local artifacts collected by Susan over the years. The installation of a stained-glass window in one of the two-bedroom cottages (cottage B1) is one of the few instances where Susan reached beyond the island style for inspiration. By building gingerbread-style cottages and painting them vibrant jewel-like tones, she sought to counteract the typical cement construction of Caribbean resorts. All of the cottages are equipped with satellite-cable television, DVD players, air-conditioning, and Jacuzzi tubs with separate showers. The bathrooms are spacious, even if somewhat dark, with copper sinks found at High Point Market, while the pillow-top mattresses are exceedingly comfortable (especially for those who have just been sleeping on boats) with sateen-finish sheets and plenty of pillows. Cottage A4 is painted a pleasant periwinkle-and-aqua-blue combination with French doors that open from the bedroom onto the terrace overlooking the view, while B2 has plenty of space. The most memorable elements of the cottages at Bel Air Plantation, though, are not the comfortable beds or even the zany paint jobs and abundance of tropical fabrics, but rather the front porches. Simple and straightforward, the verandas and their reclined seating compel the guest to do exactly what they came for—sit back and relax. For the unfussy guest who is searching for little other than laid-back comfort and relaxation in the sun with kind, hardworking hosts, then Bel Air Plantation is just the spot.

CLOCKWISE FROM TOP LEFT *Coordinated pastels on a cottage porch; a local favorite, Bel Air's waterside restaurant; island art mixes with American country furnishings found at High Point's annual furniture fair; simple, soft décor mask the unbelievably comfortable beds.*

OPPOSITE PAGE *Bel Air's luscious pool view.*

THE IAN FLEMING VILLA, GOLDENEYE

JAMAICA

*J*ust past the bustling activity of downtown Ocho Rios (Ochi, to the locals), on the main road of Jamaica's northern coast, sit the modest stone pillars that mark the private entrance to the famed Goldeneye Resort. Originally belonging to James Bond author Ian Fleming, the secluded eighteen-acre cove is now a 52-acre exclusive resort compound with five villas, eleven new beach cottages, six

brand-new lagoon suites, plus Fleming's original villa enhanced with two more bedrooms, all owned by legendary music producer Chris Blackwell. Despite the resort's increased hosting abilities, the cove near the villa remains serene amid lush tropical gardens alongside a dramatic bluff overlooking a protected coral beach and a truly inspiring inlet lagoon. Fleming clearly had an eye for property—what was once an overgrown donkey racecourse now offers unparalleled natural scenery, including a surrounding garden filled with exotic trees. The resident gardener, Ramsay, has been on board since Fleming's day and offers garden tours during which he'll happily explain the history of some of the larger trees, the multitude of bird species that call them home, and the special Goldeneye tree-planting program, for which guests are encouraged to donate a tree and thus granted a small sign noting their gift. Walking through the garden can feel a bit like strolling Hollywood Boulevard, given the names of former donors (Johnny Depp, Harrison Ford, and Jim Carrey, to name a few). The most interesting sign, though, is the original one, which stands on the edge of the lawn of the Fleming villa and bears the

name of Prime Minister Sir Anthony Eden, who was Fleming's guest at Goldeneye for three weeks following the Suez Crisis in 1956.

The property, despite its recent expansion, is designed to blend into the verdant landscape. The intent is to create ample privacy and encourage a natural, come as-you-please approach to the vacation. Sarongs, bathing suits, and flip-flops are the favored daytime wear and the buffet-style lunch, served from 1:00 p.m to 3:00 p.m., presents a pleasant, albeit rare, opportunity to mingle with the other guests. The elevated wooden deck of the bar and gazebo dining area commands the property's best view over the lagoon and newly constructed beach. However, the presentation of it all is determinedly nonchalant. Rather than gawk loudly in front of the subdued, cool crowd, it may feel more appropriate to take it all in quietly and seat yourself at the simple, white deck tables as if it were all expected. Luckily, the staff, almost all Jamaican, loves seeing your enthusiasm, particularly Clayton, the resort's friendly waiter/bartender and resident man-about-town. Clayton's quick smile and signature "Black Lady" cocktails will have you passionately

exclaiming in no time over the property's distinct beauty. Contrasting with the gazebo's all-white palette are the brightly patterned batik napkins and place mats created by Chris's wife, Mary, who was also responsible for importing the glazed hand-painted pottery from South Africa. The lunch buffet is perhaps the best offering of Goldeneye's culinary options, with massive platters of jerk chicken, baked plantains and rice, fresh vegetables, and coconut shrimp. Unfortunately, the serve-yourself system does encourage generous second helpings. The evening meal is much quieter, with guests often sticking to their villas for privately catered meals. Breakfast is also served in the villas, meaning there's no set schedule and the cups of deliciously strong Jamaican Blue Mountain coffee begin and end whenever you want.

Given Chris's musical bent, each villa is equipped with state-of-the-art stereo systems and a collection of Island Records' top CDs. Despite the enormous success of Bob Marley and its effect on Chris's career (he was the initial purchaser of the property after Fleming let it go), there is precious little Marley iconography around the property. The main reception area doubles as a DVD-rental station that features every Bond movie as well as current hits. The focus at the resort is to unwind and chill out. The main building also contains a small shop where you can purchase batik items, including the robes, place mats, and towels found in the Fleming villa.

ROOMS

If a true hideaway element is what you're after, then the Ian Fleming villa is the ultimate choice. Tucked back from the other guest villas and with its own pool, separate screening room, and most importantly, a beach in a small cove, the Fleming villa offers the most seclusion and the most astounding views over the bluff at Goldeneye. Despite its long history of glamorous guests, (Katharine Hepburn, Errol Flynn, Donald Sutherland, Cecil Beaton, Sir Laurence Olivier) the villa's structure and indeed, its very essence, is pointedly Spartan. Conceived by Fleming himself, the villa is a one-story ranch house, originally comprised of only one long room with large cutout windows constructed sans glass and designed to frame the view. The villa's simplicity was ideal for Fleming, allowing him to shut himself in and write thirteen of the Bond novels. Since Chris's reign, however, the villa has been spruced up with enormous potted ginger flowers, bamboo couches, easy chairs with batik cushions, and African artifacts, as well as two more bedrooms spanning the back of the villa. Outdoor meals at the villa, particularly breakfast, are set up to be limitless events. With the meals being served on a round white picnic table (with room for six) underneath an archway of seagrape trees at the patio on the edge of the bluff directly overlooking the sea, the setting is beyond captivating, while the shade from the trees is per-fectly cool. According to Clayton, it's hardly rare for a guest to spend three hours at the "breakfast table"—it was a beloved spot for Fleming, too. Dinners are equally entrancing with low citronella candles lining the patio and overhead lanterns dangling from the trees. Each of the villa's three bedrooms comes with spacious outdoor bathing areas with perhaps the most alluring outdoor bathtubs and showers in the Caribbean. What separates this outdoor bathing spot from the many others is its well-balanced approach between nature and luxury. Enclosed by tall bamboo fencing, the green, claw-foot tubs blend seamlessly into the leafy garden patio area while the rain showers peek out from tall bamboo plants. Stone-slab sink basins with raffia-framed mirrors add an element of style. Fortunately, the toilet component plus another sink and shower are located inside, within the rooms' en suite bathrooms—far preferable for those middle-of-the-night trips. To enjoy a bubble bath surrounded by palms, a cacophony of tree frogs, and candlelight (bath gel and candles both placed handily alongside the bathtub) is an unforgettable au naturel indulgence.

It would be impossible to describe the Fleming villa and not highlight the master bedroom's enormous bamboo bed with its separate pillared canopy. Rather than have four posters rising up from the corners of the king-plus-size mattress to create the mosquito-net canopy, the muslin is instead draped over a freestanding bamboo pergola set two feet away from either side of the bed. The result is one of the more elegantly appointed forts I've ever slept in, particularly with embroidered polka-dot sheets. Upon returning to the room after turn-down service, you'll find a scented mosquito candle flickering in the room, the bed's initial fifteen pillows reduced to three and the folding jalousie shutters tightly closed. However, I recommend opening them back up. After all, there's no threat of mosquitoes penetrating the curtained lair or the curtains sticking to your body, and above all, one of the joys of the location is waking up to the open view of sea.

Goldeneye is one of the last remaining resorts where the relaxed vibe is practically enforced. To be seen in jogging gear or really in any state of overexertion would be against the very essence of the spot. And although equipment for water sports such as kayaks and Jet Skis are available (and often used) and there is a sign directing you toward various walking trails, none of these activities seem designed with sweating in mind. The purpose of this stylish retreat is just that—to retreat from pressure and obligation. As the Jamaicans say, "Relax, mon."

The Rasta-colored décor of the villa's media room.

CLOCKWISE FROM TOP LEFT   *The villa's simple, low-slung design; the beloved breakfast table under the trees; casual comfort abounds at the Ian Fleming's villa; a bamboo canopy frame befitting two kings.*

ITOPIA

....

JAMAICA

*B*uried deep in the remote hills of Jamaica's north coast above Runaway Bay is the historically and culturally pivotal Itopia villa. Part of Jamaica's Island Outpost collection, which owns iconic beachside hotels like Jakes and the Caves in Negril, Itopia presents a totally different stature and type of property. Unlike bohemian seaside hotels, the Itopia villa is a seventeenth-century limestone house that was once the home of one of Oliver Cromwell's sixteen regents (in fact, the only one to survive when they were targeted to be killed in 1660). Today the property's regal background takes some effort to imagine, given the over-grown surroundings and hilltop location above Runaway Bay; however, the surviving stone lily pond, elegant gabled roof, and Georgian-style windows (which were either ahead of their time or refashioned in later years) lend a distinctly colonial feel to the house. When Jamaican-born author and filmmaker Perry Henzell, along with his wife Sally, also Jamaican born, bought the house it was in quite a state of neglect. Nevertheless, Sally's heralded talent for interior design quickly turned it into a haven in the hills where Perry could write in peace and Sally could paint. As intended, the house became a creative sanctuary but not for Perry and Sally alone. Instead the house became a regular meeting place for talented icons of the 1970s music and literary scene, including Steve Winwood, Joni Mitchell, and Jimmy Cliff, who were all friends and colleagues of Perry and Sally. Best known for his film *The Harder They Come,* starring Jimmy Cliff, the first-ever feature film made in Jamaica, the late Perry Henzell is a legend within his country for championing the rights of the oppressed, while his connection to reggae came through his close childhood friend, Chris Blackwell. There is an almond tree in the backyard that covers a picnic table and a rusted old grill, which, according to Sally, was host to many a long Sunday lunch shared among some of the most well-known names in music. Walking around the property today, the aura of creative inspiration is palpable. Whether it is the crumbling stone and ivy-covered façade or the curious sea-glass balls that hang from the rafters of the studio where Perry's office remains relatively untouched, the evidence of distinct historical significance is readily apparent in both the house's exterior and interior. It's little surprise that Sally has found a collection of buried personal effects on the property including glass dolls, pipes, buttons, and even a knife with an ivory handle.

And then there's the interior of the house. Simply laid out with three small bedrooms and a hodgepodge of antique furnishings, local artwork, and Sally's porcelain collectibles, the villa claims no pronounced interior design (other than a celebration of life's passing) or elegant trimmings. Instead, the walls of the front hall and living room have been left alone to age and peel with grace, revealing a wonderfully natural and striking palette of blues, beiges, yellows, and browns that no paint job could ever create. They also offset the original bulletwood plank floors (so strong only homemade nails will work) and an elegant Adams sideboard inherited from Perry's family. As Sally adoringly refers to their home, "It's like living in a painting." The décor of the living room is further testament to Sally's multicultural history and love of art—the Burmese dancers in bronze are from a past trip, the Chinese Buddha by the door is because of Sally's mother's heritage, while the two large paintings are done by Jamaican painter Graham Davis and Cuban artist Fardo. The furniture, mostly handed down from Perry's and Sally's families, bears English and West Indian designs while the fabric on the one mahogany-backed sofa looks Victorian and feels and looks every bit as historic as the rest of the place. The concept of time is entirely lost once you've stepped into the villa. The necessity for today's high-end comforts seems wholly superficial and the Thoreau-esque lifestyle feels well within reach at Itopia. It's no wonder that the owners bill it as the ideal artist's retreat. The downstairs features two bedrooms on either side of the small back kitchen, and a dining room that opens onto the stone patio overlooking the gardens. The villa is neither small nor large but then again, it's not meant to fit into any typical category. The name is a hybrid of "Ethiopia" and "Utopia" and was Sally's idea to reference the house's humility and greatness. The staff of two, Eufemia the cook and Karl the gardener, are sweet natured and helpful. Eufemia makes a mean calaloo dish

The mesmerizing palette of the living room walls display a simple, natural progression of color.

BELOW   *Looking into a butter-yellow guest room with antique secretary desk, once belonging to the famous Jamaican activist and friend of the owner, Marcus Garvey.*

TOP TO BOTTOM
*The owners' hand-me-down antiques in
the living room; the verdant main entrance.*

with snapper and salad, though may need some instruction on just how continental you prefer your meals, particularly breakfast, during which, if you're not explicit, you're likely to get the Jamaican staple of ackee and saltfish. If you're willing to taste full Jamaican fare, then there's no more authentic spot or chef. Meals are served either in the house's cozy ground floor dining room or outside under the trees. Itopia is not for the faint of heart or for those looking for a plush beach vacation. This is an experience in all its sensory glory. If the Rastas' Ital lifestyle has ever fascinated you, but not quite enough to drive you into the hills, then a stay at the Itopia villa will make for the ideal baby step.

ROOMS

There are three simple bedrooms at Itopia, each with queen-sized beds, plus a daybed in the studio's library. Given the house's original structure, all indoor plumbing had to be added relatively recently and so the villa's two bathrooms exemplify a contemporary look and style of the 1970s. The top floor bedroom is the most private with butter-yellow walls, two large windows, and a sizable walk-in shower in the bathroom en suite. The sky-blue desk in the corner actually belonged to Marcus Garvey, the founder of Jamaica's Pan-Africanism movement, proving yet another impressive tie between Itopia and Jamaican history. The mattress in the upstairs bedroom is springy and decorated with mismatched

sheets and a patchwork quilt. There is a red light on the outside of the house that casts a bright red glow to the room. The two bedrooms downstairs are pleasant, though only one has a bathroom en suite—and a full-length mural painted by none other than Joni Mitchell. The rooms are all of equal size, though the "Joni Mitchell room" has a sunken bathtub in its whimsical pink, seashell-adorned bathroom. Nevertheless, I prefer the bedroom without a bathroom for its simple white bedding, four-poster canopy bed and antique, oval mirror. Surprisingly, the house does have Wi-Fi, and cable television can be found in the studio's library, not that you'll find yourself watching it. Sleeping at Itopia is a curious event that requires a relaxed mindset—luckily, that's easy to come by in Jamaica. The numerous stray dogs can be heard taunting one another throughout the night and the roosters really do crow at first light. In fitting with a historic house, both in essence and current standing, there are no screens on the windows, though thankfully mosquito nets are dangling over the beds. To enjoy your stay at the Itopia villa, you must have your expectations well set beforehand. The villa is unlike any other and its history and sense of place are what compels it as a hideaway and spot worth visiting. The character of the house—earned through its tremendously inspiring inhabitants— is the draw of the house. For a peek into a real and renowned Jamaican artist's life, there's no better place.

CLOCKWISE FROM TOP LEFT *A decorated corner of the living room; the owners' collection of curios on careful display; the Poseidon–themed ground–floor bathroom; a precious antique sideboard from Perry Henzell's family.*

OPPOSITE PAGE *The weathered stone façade of the former English country house.*

KANOPI HOUSE

· · · · · · · · · · · · · ·

JAMAICA

*L*ocated in perhaps the most inspiring spot in all of Jamaica, the newly constructed tree-house cabins of Kanopi House hover over the infamous Blue Lagoon (yes, the very one that brought Brooke Shields from baby face to womanhood) on the island's eastern tip in Port Antonio. Known as "Porty" or "Portland" to the locals, Port Antonio is the former playpen of Golden Age

Hollywood (Greta Garbo, Errol Flynn) but has fallen into dilapidation since the cruise ships turned away in the late 1980s. Recently, however, the area has seen pronounced interest from a few wealthy hotel developers plus the arrival of Geejam, a modern-style boutique property with its own professional-grade recording studio and curious sushi-jerk fusion restaurant. As a result, the area has been creeping back onto the radar, drawing adventurous travelers eager for something beyond touristy Montego Bay and Negril to its natural beauty and host of activities including rafting down the Rio Grande, Jamaica's largest river, and hiking to waterfalls in the jungle-thick Blue Mountains.

At Kanopi House, the involvement with the natural surroundings is immediate and, frankly, unavoidable. The closest thing to a bona fide Swiss Family Robinson hideaway, Kanopi House offers that distinct type of holiday when the second you arrive, you're certain it will be unlike any other vacation before or after. Built right into the hillside over the Blue Lagoon, the six tree house-style cottages, including the manager's house, sit apart from one another, each with their own distinctive view of the lagoon. Built in an eco-friendly, low impact manner, Kanopi House is proud

to have felled zero trees during its construction; rather, buildings were adjusted to accommodate nature. Thick with chartreuse bamboo and towering banyan trees, the hillside is a veritable jungle and thus its natural inhabitants are only an arm's length away (so those not into Mother Nature's crawling, chirping, and buzzing creatures may want to turn the page). The fauna is so thick on the property that from some angles the tree houses do really seem to be dangling from the trees. Built by the owners of Kamalame Cay, a beach-style hideaway in the Bahamas, Kanopi House is the dream project of Jamaican-born builder Brian Hew and his interior-designer wife, Jennifer. A family affair, Kanopi House is overseen by their son, David, and managed by Brian's childhood friend and local Porty resident, Michael Fox. The five guest accommodations were all built by local artisans, and are elegant yet simple structures of blond and dark mahogany and cedar wood connected by a stone pathway that climbs up and down the hillside, which, funnily enough, makes for a great jogging circuit.

The camplike compound lends itself well to a relaxed vacation among friends and family. Kanopi's main cottage is the definitive gathering point, with an open-air living and dining room

area that's inviting at all hours. With its louvered windows, sliding glass doors and impressive mahogany-beam canopy roof, the main cabin is not only the most attractive of the cabins but also offers the best view of the lagoon and its crumbling mansion row. Its cushioned wicker chairs and mahogany settees make for comfortable lounging while the cool breezes running through the cabin catch the ceiling fans and keep the Swiss Family Robinson aspect at full tilt. Meals are served at the main cabin's two circular mahogany tables that are often pushed together, since the property lends itself to mingling, and is often rented exclusively by groups of ten. The hostess of Kanopi, Karla, a Belgian with impressive dreadlocks, and the on-site manager, Michael, run the day-to-day operations, organizing everything from daily meals to various desired excursions (Rio Grande, Scatter Falls, Geejam's bar and restaurant, or the area's famous local beaches like Frenchman's Cove, San San, or Winnifred Beach). The discreet kitchen staff is on hand to prepare everything from the commonly requested eggs-and-bacon breakfast to the Jamaican saltfish-and-plantain version. The vegetables are straight from Michael's hillside garden and the fish is bought fresh each day. Be sure to ask for a batch of the cook's festivals (Jamaican hush puppies) for breakfast or a snack—they're absurdly delicious and satisfy that delicious, vacation-only permittance for indulgence. A highlight is a memorable meal cooked and served in the outdoor barbecue area that is styled like an African *boma* (actually conceived after the Hews' family vacation to Africa) with a smattering of

The main cottage lit up for cocktails.

PREVIOUS PAGES
*Tucked into the jungle-like hills,
Kanopi defines tree-house seclusion.*

OPPOSITE PAGE
Kanopi's wild shoreline on the Blue Lagoon.

Adirondack chairs around a big fire pit, surrounded by flickering tiki torches. The property has its own private shoreline on the lagoon with a protected swimming hole and view out towards the sea that includes a curious uninhabited jungle island. The small pebble beach is littered with Adirondack chairs and strewn kayaks, tempting the guests, particularly in the afternoon when it gets full sun. Be sure to kayak to the island during the day for an exotic exploration-style adventure and then cruise down the row of dilapidated waterfront mansions along the lagoon's eastern edge—Porty's famed Gold Coast. Despite the faded glory of the majority of houses along the lagoon's edge, the setting proclaims a distinct beauty with its truly azure waters and verdant, untamed landscape making the houses appear even more beautiful in their neglect. It's as if nature eventually won. Also, do not miss the chance to borrow the house canoe for a moonlit paddle through the nearby brackish inlet and witness the mesmerizing nighttime phosphorescence from the inhabiting organisms.

ROOMS

The five guest tree houses at Kanopi vary in size and style. Some mimic the main cabin with full mahogany builds and sliding glass doors, while others have painted cedar-plank siding and upside-down layouts (where the living room is above the bedroom). All of the cabins, though, are Jamaican-built and include louvered, cedar window shutters, elegant, locally, handmade furnishings such as carved, four-poster beds and plantation-style chairs, and Spanish elm and sweet wood floors. Kanopi is quite mindful of its surrounding community, choosing to rely heavily on local artisans to not only furnish the cottages but also create its accessories, such as laundry and waste baskets woven from Jamaican banana leaf. The owners' cabin, Almond Tree, is the largest of the guest cottages with a queen-size mahogany bed set up to face the wide front porch and the expansive view of the lagoon beyond. The second largest, Upper Deck, has the highest perch of the cabins, offering a king-of-the-hill-type perspective over the entire property and lagoon. For those with small children, Sweetwood's two bedrooms, small kitchenette, full living room, and porch area make it the most self-sufficient and comfortable option. The cabins are all fairly similar with regard to bathrooms, most offering showers rather than baths and although slightly rustic (judging from the luxury standard of things), they are beyond comfortable for what is truly needed.

Nevertheless, sleeping at Kanopi may take some getting used to. The evening noises are abundant, from cricket and tree-frog symphonies to branches brushing in the wind and the lagoon lapping. Although it all is ridiculously idyllic, when mixed together the sounds can be loud and require some adjustment. The other thing to note is the lack of shades in the bedroom, so expect to be woken with the sun. However, the rooms have comfortable, firm mattresses, air-conditioning for those who must have it, and quilted linens from Ralph Lauren. The Kanopi House is, without a doubt, best suited for those willing to sacrifice creature comforts for comfort alongside creatures. The cabins offer rustic luxury in an upscale-camping-style environment. Kanopi's style of living is meant to encourage direct communication with nature and to appreciate the rich surroundings. I implore you to go see the wilder side of Jamaica, and ultimately, experience the authenticity and benefit of immersing oneself in a fascinating landscape and culture.

The languid interiors of the tree-house-style main cottage.

CLOCKWISE FROM TOP LEFT   *The casual sitting room of the duplex cottage; a secret garden within Kanopi's jungle surroundings; the master cottage's suite–like layout; a hand–carved blond mahogany bed awaits.*

POINT OF VIEW, TRYALL CLUB

JAMAICA

A former sugar plantation, the fifty-year-old, gated Tryall Club spreads out over 2,200 acres of oceanfront and lush mountain terrain on the northern coast of Jamaica, just forty-five minutes from Montego Bay (depending on the road conditions, of course). The original nineteenth-century Georgian-style great house still stands, atop a manicured hill, presiding over the championship

eighteen-hole golf course (and former host of the Johnny Walker World Championship) and white sandy beach below. The resort features seventy-two (and growing) privately owned properties that can be rented through the club's reservation office; they range from one-bedroom suites at the great house to decadent eight-bedroom hilltop villas, complete with full staff. The trick is finding the right villa that allows you to relax instantly, appreciate the wonderful amenities of Tryall, and enjoy the sanctuary of your own private space. I believe Point of View to be one of the best, if not the best, in terms of décor, view, and overall comfort.

Tucked way back in the resort, proudly stationed at the top of the highest hill, Point of View villa commands one of the best views and stately positions on Jamaica's northwestern coast. Wisely angled toward the setting sun, its long multi-pillared veranda is stuffed with various sitting and dining areas to drink in the expansive view of the sea and the neighboring jungle valley and mountainous hills. Given that Tryall faces more north than west, the view of the sunset is often compromised by a protruding hill on the left. Point of View, however, is situated high enough that it seems to keep the glorious pink light on

its face for just a bit longer than any of the other villas. The location, on a precipice over a knee-weakening deep valley, is also unique in Tryall and offers an entirely different view into the untamed natural beauty of Jamaica.

Tryall immediately lends itself to the active types, going beyond golf with a modern tennis center, recently renovated fitness area with updated equipment and yoga classes on the deck, croquet, volleyball and basketball down at the beach, plus all water sports. My favorite, though, is the Tryall Fun Run marked out along the winding paved roads of the resort with painted yellow feet that have since faded in the blistering sun. (Don't miss the finale of climbing the stairs in front of the great house—they're the bragging rights at the end of your jog and they conveniently end right at the porch of the great house bar.) Tryall's affable and welcoming demeanor makes it easy for newcomers to visit the property, even though it is a private club with overseas memberships and legions of longtime visitors.

Driving up the hilly driveway to the pebble-laid carport (saved for golf carts, the preferred mode of transportation at Tryall) Point of View's shingled pagoda entrance is first to appear. Its latticed walls and potted palms create an

auspicious entrance, which is heightened by the cage of chirping parakeets hanging inside. The elegant arrival continues on the other side of the pagoda as a cut-limestone path emerges from clipped green grass and an Asian-inspired waterfall creates the sound of rushing water. Blooming orange and pink ginger flowers in the side garden and iron tiki torches set the stage for the centerpiece, an Indonesian bench littered with bright orange and blue pillows. From there the guest must make a sharp right turn to enter the house's main parlor room, though given one's newfound relaxed state, it hardly feels jarring. The entrance to Point of View is so thoughtfully composed that it stands testament to the importance of an arrival and its ability to set the tone of the entire house.

The front parlor room is light and airy with opposing sets of four handsome, mahogany-based French doors that open out to the veranda. The room's vaulted ceiling features two antique gold and aqua-blue-painted chandeliers that fairly "pop" on account of the cream-colored walls and matching polished limestone floors. Two Jamaican woven rugs lie underneath identical English floral-upholstered sofa and chair sets, which are stylishly accented by crackle paint-treated coffee tables and red porcelain drums. The room is functional, with a flat-screen television in a built-in armoire, but the more alluring lounge area, the real hub of activity, is out on the long veranda where locally made mahogany furniture by Jamaican designers Prince Palmer and Paul Mathieu create a comfortable and relaxed setting. The veranda, seeming more like a loggia,

PREVIOUS PAGE   *The trellised pagoda entryway at Point of View.*

ABOVE   *A pleasantly sophisticated veranda.*

Uncomplicated, classic style in the living room.

encompasses the entire length of the house and features cushioned sitting areas off each of the five bedrooms. In the center of the loggia is a large lounge complete with 1950s-style dark furniture with canvas cushions by Perennials, an inlaid-marble wet bar, and a card table plus a long dining room table that seats up to eighteen. The rectangular, imported coral-stone pool is yet another focal point of the house, along with its decorative Moroccan lanterns and mahogany lounge chairs under white market umbrellas done by local favorite Prince Palmer. Despite its single story, the house features multiple eaves and high ceilings, which are a mark of the lauded architect Kasimir Korybut, known for his prowess with West Indian style. He is also credited with the customized balustrade that connects the roof with the veranda's white pillars, offering both a clear passage for the breeze to filter through the long, covered veranda and an attractive aesthetic element to the exterior design. Given the house's fluid layout, high-end materials, and elevated level of décor, the villa is ideal for cocktail parties and large group dinner parties. What makes it even better is that it's also ideal for quiet and private relaxation, particularly in the early morning when the mist consumes the neighboring valley, giving the entire property an ethereal glow. The combination of the hazy jungle and the glittering sea makes the view during your first cup of coffee the most serene of the day.

ROOMS

The five bedrooms of Point of View (along with the forthcoming second master suite currently in planning stages) are all superbly well appointed with quality American and English fabrics, four-poster beds, and French-style mahogany furniture. Decorated by local designer Sue Williams, who has used her vast network of Jamaican artisans to do villas at neighboring resort Round Hill as well as at Tryall, Point of View is where she made sure that Jamaica and its lush surroundings provided the overall inspiration. Decadent bathrooms are yet another distinction of the Point of View villa in comparison to other villas at Tryall—excluding the more recent ones built behind the golf course's back nine, which have introduced a defiant splashiness to the once modest resort. With stand-alone soaking tubs surrounded by louvered mahogany windows, and separated double vanities stocked with Jo Malone products, the bathrooms present a far more tailored and upscale approach than the Tryall norm (almost boutique hotel-like). The more interesting element, though, is the carved mahogany swinging doors that enclose the toilet areas in each bathroom. Delicate and

whimsical designs of palm trees and pineapples bring back a tropical influence to the otherwise polished home. The current master suite is at the far left end of the house, closest to the driveway but, despite its sophisticated mahogany furnishings and Bennison linen fabrics, it is not my favorite room in the villa. Instead, the newly designed master suite off the right side of the house, with soaring views over the thick jungle valley and out to sea, is my pick as the ultimate room at Tryall. Its outdoor bamboo shower is completely open to the plummeting valley below, which requires some getting used to, but by the second or third day, trepidation gives way to easy fantasies of showering in a jungle waterfall. Fortunately all the rooms have panoramic views of the sea and their own cushioned seating areas. The house lends itself well to various types of groups and families by offering numerous private corners, a large lawn and pool area, plus décor that impresses as much as it comforts. For a stylish villa that will ensure your cocktail party is the talk of the Tryall season, book Point of View and start planning.

OPPOSITE PAGE   *The lantern–adorned pool just before sunset.*

ABOVE, CLOCKWISE FROM TOP LEFT   *The loggia style of the veranda; the enviable sunset view; the carefully chosen fabrics of the master bedroom; charming, carved mahogany doors in the master bathroom.*

ROUND HILL HOTEL AND VILLAS

MONTEGO BAY, JAMAICA

*T*ucked into a hillside blissfully separated from the busy main road, Round Hill's twenty-seven villas and Ralph Lauren-designed hotel rooms offer desirable seclusion in a sophisticated and private setting. Positioned around a calm horseshoe-shaped bay and protected from winds, Round Hill's cottages, as they're known, are still every bit the tightly bonded, exclusive compound

its original designers intended. Once the pineapple-shaped gatehouse has raised its long lever, admitting you onto the palm-fringed, sloping driveway, you have the overwhelming sensation that you've arrived among the land of the privileged. As the road bends, passing white jalousied cottages and glistening, Har-Tru tennis courts, the anticipation builds. Fortunately, the hotel's whitewashed entrance, classically adorned with green-and-white striped canopies, doesn't disappoint. For over fifty years, Round Hill has been noted for its refined presentation, and after just two minutes of standing on the checkerboard marble front porch overlooking the sparkling sea, you'll have little reason to disagree.

Despite Round Hill's storied reputation, the hotel has responded to current luxury demands by adding a signature spa, wisely set away from the bustling beach and lunch deck area, with Elemis products and daily yoga classes, plus a new infinity pool with attentive bar service and Beverly Hills Hotel-style pergolas. A family-oriented spot, Round Hill is a haven for tennis players, with its five courts and a cherished pro who arranges its popular tennis programs. There's also a litany of water sports like kayaking, sailing with Hobie Cats, and tubing, snorkeling, and scuba trips, all

available upon request. The spa's gym is well equipped but space is a bit tight, so it's best to use the gym at the less-favored midday hour. The kid's club is especially popular among guests and is the reason many families continue to return, while weekly entertainment programs including art shows, dance performances, and beach buffets keep adult guests delightfully amused. Like any family-friendly spot, the hotel tends to get the most crowds over Christmas vacations and spring breaks. It is during these highly trafficked times that the spa's removed location and reserved "tranquil area" of chaise longues and hammocks are most appreciated. Be sure to book your spa appointments well ahead of time though, and not during scheduled fitness classes, since they take place right below some of the treatment rooms and can be distracting.

The hotel's main dining is located on a shaded seaside terrace that sits in front of the bar. Another restaurant, used mainly for private events and formal dinner, is located above the terrace overlooking the entire property. The Jamaican-tinged continental cuisine has just been improved upon with a new James Beard–honored chef, whose jerk chicken rice-paper rolls are fast becoming travel incentives unto their own.

Round Hill's pièce de résistance, however, is actually one of its oldest elements—its elegant bar. Designed by Round Hill's most celebrated home-owner, Ralph Lauren, the navy-and-white-striped cushioned banquettes are the epitome of Lauren's preppy American classic design. Complemented by gleaming mahogany bar tables and chairs, carved white columns, simple brass sconces, and black-and-white framed prints of old Hollywood glamour, the bar's timeless beauty offers one of the Caribbean's better incentives for you to don your top tropical outfit. The bar's entrance is through a curtained veranda decorated with low-slung table-and-chair sets done in what can best be described as the Jamaican version of the Adirondack chair style. Their chic, curved design and high-gloss white paint is highly imitable and comfortably caters to everything from daily tea service to evening cocktails. The terrace and bar area, though, displays its true essence just after dinner, when the bar's piano player is at work and the center dinner tables on the terrace have been cleared away, making way for impromptu moonlit slow dancing.

ROOMS

Divided among thirty-six hotel rooms, twenty-seven cottages, and a select offering of larger rental villas with full use of Round Hill amenities, the accommodation options are plentiful. The hotel rooms are housed in what's called the Pineapple House, a two-story building with suites on the first and second floors, all with sea views, while the lower-level rooms also have terraces. Recently refurbished by none other than Ralph himself, the rooms exhibit a contemporary, Caribbean style in an all-white palette with four-poster bamboo beds and accent red-and-navy-striped pillows. Despite Ralph's signature clean lines, crisp new linens, and modern bathrooms, the rooms can feel a bit cramped, especially if you plan to stay for more than a weekend. They are directly over the pool and beach area, which can be loud during peak season. Also, be sure to book the lower-level rooms since their terraces offer desirable extra square footage; note that the rooms along the far end have the most privacy. Given the initial community-minded premise of Round Hill, the cottages tend to be the more pleasing choice for staying, though you should be equally as specific when booking with regard to location. Individually owned but managed by Round Hill, the cottages offer a wide variety of options for size, décor, and setting. The larger cottages, with up to four bedrooms, can be rented as a whole or split between guests—be sure to check prior to booking whether you are sharing with others. I recommend taking a smaller cottage, like cozy, three-bedroom cottage 12 or, if you are a larger group, then cottage 17, which has been recently redesigned by local designer Sue Williams. Cottage 12 is owned by the family of the shoe designer-cum-hotelier Vanessa Noel. Not unlike her fanciful shoe designs, the interiors of cottage 12 are vibrant, exotic, and unabashedly cosmopolitan. Gem-colored pillows of raw silk adorn the living room's casual bamboo furnishings as well as the tall, four-poster mahogany beds. The two top rooms have their own identical, marble bathrooms en suite, making the preference between the two even more slight. However, the farther room is set back more and opens into a small sitting room, making it feel more private. The lower-level room is a bit cavernous, given its location right off the cottage's stairs, and

better suited for those who prefer their coming and going to be less easily monitored (read: teenagers). The cottage is marked by bright contrasts like the deep red wall in the sitting room, the cheetah-print ottoman, and the cherished paintings of late local artist (and former British television star) Jonathan Routh. The most impressive piece in the house, though, is the eight-person imperial-style dark-stained dining table and chairs set up against the porch railing and commanding a stunning view over the kidney-shaped pool and hot-pink bougainvillea bush to the sea below. A focal point of the cottage's interior design, the table sets the stylish, convivial tone of the house. For those looking to escape with a friend or even to indulge and take the whole cottage for yourself, cottage 12 is the style maven's savvy choice. For a larger group or family vacation, I recommend the fresh look of cottage 17, whose smart, contemporary décor presents a relaxing and tasteful backdrop to a stay at Round Hill. Its secluded location at the top of the hill allows for uninterrupted views of the resort and the northwestern coastline of Jamaica. Even better, the bedrooms are spacious, one with the same bamboo bed as the hotel's rooms. The rooms also feature West Indian plantation-style furnishings and mahogany floors as well as gorgeous new bathrooms. The rooms are well designed for groups, with king-size or twin beds and locations on three different floors. Another even more decadent option is one of the two grand villas that sit at the very top of Round Hill, both of which can be rented through Jamaica Villas by Linda Smith and come with memberships to both Round Hill and the neighboring Tryall Golf Club. Longview Manor, my favorite of the two villas, is ideal for multiple families, multi-generational reunions, or better yet, a fabulous and unforgettable party. From its commanding position, the views are truly

expansive, capturing the sunrise and sunset plus the lush Blue Mountains and the twinkling lights of Mo' Bay. With over 2,000 square feet of veranda space plus almost an acre of flowering land, the dimensions are even more impressive when filled with people. Add to that a private tennis court, swimming pool, and a separate guest cottage with three more bedrooms (making for a total of seven bedrooms), and you've got all the trappings of an over-the-top villa vacation, and as it is all encased in the private confines of Round Hill, seclusion is ensured. The interiors of Longview are slightly disappointing given the magnitude of possibility; however, details like white marble floors, green-and-white striped awnings over twelve sets of French doors, and modern wicker furniture on the veranda keep it pleasant and, ultimately, comfortably unobtrusive. The master bedroom attempts to offer some décor savoir-faire with an elegant four-poster bed covered with a cream linen drapery. The master bathroom, though, is where the architect must have seen himself most. Not only is it enormous, it has a separate, spa-like shower room with a pocket window looking out into frangipani trees. The cottage rooms are more comfortable than their counterparts in the main house, enjoying more intimate views, brighter fabric selections, and a better layout overall. Nevertheless, all the seven rooms have bathrooms en suite, ample closet space, and brand new mattresses. The villa's best asset, though, may be Marcia, the resident cook, whose cooking ranges from French toast à la bananas flambé to extra-spicy jerk chicken. So, if there's a worthy celebration approaching, and a fully-loaded hilltop villa in an exclusive resort in Jamaica seems like a fitting backdrop, then there may be no better recommendation than Longview Manor. I can assure you that all invited guests will be eternally grateful.

PREVIOUS PAGES *Looking out towards Montego Bay from Longview Villa's hilltop position.*

ABOVE, FROM LEFT TO RIGHT *The curved version of the classic Adirondack chair at Round Hill's infamous bar; awaiting your rum-punch order at the beach bar.*

A chic, safari-print fabric jazzes up a bedroom in cottage 12.

CLOCKWISE FROM TOP LEFT *Dramatic canopy bed curtains in the master bedroom at Longview Manor; a Quadrille fabric on bedroom chairs in a guest room at Longview Manor; the alfresco dining table at Longview Manor; the kidney-shaped pool at cottage 12.*

MONTPELIER PLANTATION

NEVIS

*T*ucked into the foreground of towering Nevis Peak, the nineteen-room Montpelier Plantation Inn exudes timelessness with its colonial, early eighteenth-century buildings and graceful, traditional approach. The family-run, country-style inn sits 750 feet above the sea alongside towering Mt. Nevis, offering sweeping views over the plantation's verdant, sixty-acre estate, the sea, and the island of St. Kitts beyond. Surrounded by flamboyant African tulip trees and fragrant gardens of frangipani, gardenias, and night-blooming jasmine, their scent so powerful you can almost feel them burning their memory into your brain, this country-style inn epitomizes a hideaway.

Pulling through the venerable stone pillars, past the white plantation house, up to the low great house of volcanic stone with Georgian-style windows and painted shutters, is so transporting you can't help but wish your vehicle were a horse-drawn carriage. Even though only the entrance and left side of the main house are original, dating back to 1710, the historic structure appears seamless and dignified, aided by a wandering purple vine and a low row of palms. Center stage is an enormous, forty-year-old ficus tree whose arching branches cover the entire front part of the driveway and extend back over the plantation house, which holds the reception area and quaint hotel "sugar shop." The friendly welcome, usually delivered by one of the on-site Hoffman family members, is accentuated by a fresh rum punch and a cool towel. A quick tour commences, showcasing the property's highlights: the elegantly refurbished great room; the Relais & Châteaux–affiliated terrace restaurant; and the hotel's architectural emblem, an original stone windmill-cum-private dining room. The schedule at Montpelier is very traditionally organized. Each meals is served during a set two-hour window, including tea and pre-dinner cocktails, and at night, long pants and collared shirts are the dress code for men. Those who come to Montpelier year after year appreciate its set ways and relatively peaceful quality. Although the main house has a game room and children over eight are welcome, the predominant crowd at the inn comes seeking its tranquil environment. Throughout the day, guests who choose to stay on property (most seem to venture out) can be found lounging anywhere from a poolside chaise to a cushioned chair on the stone loggia or in one of the red Adirondack chairs scattered out in the field. Montpelier by the Sea, the property's private beach club on Pinney's Beach, is serviced by a daily shuttle but it only makes one round trip, meaning the times must be agreed upon by all participating guests. For this reason, and to explore the rest of Nevis at whim (or play golf at the heralded Four Seasons), I suggest renting a car, which can be easily parked in Montpelier's ample grass lot. The Hoffmans' adorable twin yellow Labs are fixtures of the property and exemplary pillars of obedience and decorum, remaining out of the restaurant at all times and rarely, if ever, barking.

At night, when Montpelier grows remarkably dark (a hideaway bonus), flickering hurricane lamps and small cannonball-fashioned torches are lit around the property—needless to say, the effect is enchanting. The lanterns lining the cut-stone steps of the great house are enough to set any colonial-era fantasy alight. In fact, the spirit of romance is unavoidable at Montpelier and not just because the lights twinkle and the air is thick with jasmine, but also due to its romantic history as the site of Horatio Nelson's wedding to Fanny Nesbit (who was given away by Nelson's naval colleague, the future King William IV). It's no wonder that half of the hotel's business is from outside guests eager to dine at the renowned terrace restaurant or inside the magnificent walls of the 300-year-old windmill. As a result, in-house guests must alert reception daily to their dining schedule to ensure tables are held. Climbing the stone stairs toward the barrel-ceilinged great room for evening cocktails, dressed in your finest, is the exact type of Old World, almost cinematic, elegance that compels couples to visit the islands.

PREVIOUS PAGE   *The timeless entrance that once hosted horse-drawn carriages of Montpelier Plantation.*

OPPOSITE PAGE   *Modern furnishings decorate the lounge area of the historic manor house.*

BELOW, FROM TOP TO BOTTOM   *The eighteenth-century windmill; the pastoral grounds and hilltop view of Montpelier Plantation.*

ROOMS

The nineteen rooms at Montpelier are split into three categories, spread broadly around the garden property and connected by a meandering garden path. Housed in low-slung cottages that almost betray the historic character of the main building with their contemporary style, the rooms are, nevertheless, fresh and comfortably appointed. The Plantation rooms, the deluxe room category, are an easy, basic choice with polished wooden floors, minifridges, private outdoor terraces, and renovated bathrooms with mahogany vanities, vessel sinks, and generous amounts of Elemis products. (Poor Tim Hoffman incorrectly thought the large bottles would discourage guests from taking them home.) The next category up is the newer (as of October 2008) Garden Suite, number 20, whose feather in its cap is an exceptionally soft four-poster bed with a curious bamboo-reed headboard. A private garden terrace features a cushioned gazebo lounge littered with pillows, providing an intimate hamlet overlooking the rolling hill and the sea beyond. White walls, streaked bamboo floors, and luminous colors (like a sunny yellow sofa with red throw pillows) give the room a bright, natural feel. The open, split-level layout allows for a nicely cooling breeze to circulate from the sliding

glass doors in the sunken sitting room all the way back to the double walk-in shower behind the bed wall. At night, when strong enough, the trade winds rattle the windows, making the rooms feel extra cozy inside. Up-to-date amenities include a Nespresso machine and iPod docking station, though purposely there are no televisions, in the hopes people will appreciate the surroundings instead. Yet, for those who simply can't forgo television, the top-level suite, a two-bedroom villa, number 21, has a television with DVD player plus a private plunge pool and sun deck. The two bedrooms are of equal size and square shape with louvered windows, darling embroidered bedding, and walk-in rain showers. Alas, they aren't as spacious as one would prefer and therefore are really best reserved for sleeping only. Like the Garden Suite's, the center living room has a wet bar, Nespresso coffee machine, and stereo system. Both new rooms also have Wi-Fi access. Overall, the rooms at Montpelier Plantation play second fiddle to the traditional main house and romantic dining experience; however, after a full day of eating, lounging, and exploring, the most important task is to get a good night's sleep, and with the new mattresses in all of the rooms listed above, that's guaranteed.

Dinner for two at the hotel's Relais & Châteux restaurant.

ABOVE, CLOCKWISE FROM TOP LEFT   *The pool's sun porch and resident guard dog; the adjacent carriage house, home to the gift shop and check-in; a bamboo headboard in one of the recently refurbished guest cottages; the windmill set up for a private dinner.*

THE HERMITAGE

NEVIS

A collection of pastel-painted gingerbread cottages, the Hermitage, a plantation inn, is one of the most prized gems of Nevis (known as the Queen of the Caribbean), favored for its genuine West Indian style. Vibrant against the lush green lawn of the eight-acre property, the scattered cottages, all with white trim, shuttered windows, and tin roofs, typify tropical simplicity.

Arriving at the property involves a few sharp turns and steep climbs—in typical hideaway fashion—but the reward is a memorable first impression filled with historic charm. The long, bumpy driveway leads past the owners' horse stables and antique carriages, a stone cistern amid grassy lawns with towering palms and mango trees, and ends in a circular area in front of a narrow, two-story shingled reception area with blue-and-white painted shutters. The property's great house is rumored to be the oldest wooden house in the Caribbean, having been built around 1680. From its corrugated red roof to the wood frame made from lignum vitae (a rare hardwood resistant to the elements), this 330-year-old dwelling exudes the appropriate amount of rambling authenticity. Similar to many early Caribbean homes, the house was constructed by ships' carpenters who favored crossbeam reinforcements (like those in a ship's hull), for the roofing structure. As a result, the ceilings are higher, giving the interior of the house a more open, spacious feel.

Owned and operated by the Lupinacci family, who have been on the island for forty-plus years, the Hermitage is now as much a totem to the family's history and personal style as it is the island's historic style. Transferred from Pennsylvania to St. Kitts in the

early 1960s, Richard Lupinacci bought the property when it was just two buildings and a privy. Together with his wife, Maureen, and children, Richard updated the manor house with a modern kitchen, a new paint job, including a burgundy color on the wooden floors, and new bathrooms. Next, he filled it with mahogany furniture they found in scrap heaps on the island. According to Richard, they were the lucky beneficiaries of the time when people were chucking antiques in favor of Danish modern furniture. In 1983 they began to build, adding gingerbread-style cottages for friends and extended family. When the houseguest number reached an alarming fifty-six, Richard decided to turn the property into an inn. In 1985, the family opened the inn with seven rooms.

Tucked at the base of Nevis Peak, 800 feet up in the hills, the Hermitage has created its own pocket of serenity amid the natural surroundings, complemented by a freshwater pool, a hard-surface tennis court, and plenty of riding trails and nature walks. A daily beach shuttle takes guests on the fifteen-minute ride down to the property's beach club just north of the Four Seasons Hotel. Everything is ready and waiting (towels, chairs, kayaks), plus the colorful beach bar allows you to sign your charges back to your room. Given the island's

tremendous history, most guests find themselves off site during the day: Alexander Hamilton was born on the island, and a nearby collection of plantation ruins include a recently discovered slave village, plus one can visit the remarkable botanical garden, with its thousands of orchid blossoms.

Returning to the Hermitage each day is like coming home to your own quirky village compound filled with all the zany characters you'd expect. The social atmosphere at the Hermitage, set by the Lupinaccis, allows guests to easily interact, whether at afternoon tea in the hodgepodge great room with classical music in the background or over home-brewed rum punches in the intimate mahogany bar. In no time, you'll feel like a regular houseguest. The inn's lauded restaurant draws a healthy crowd of outsiders throughout the day, especially in the evening when the lattice on the dining porch glows with twinkling lights and the bullfrogs and crickets hold their nightly performance. The menu changes daily to guarantee freshness and almost all the dishes come from local producers or are made from ingredients raised on the plantation itself, and the desserts are all homemade. The five-course plantation dinner is well worth the occasional, not-so-pleasant, exotic flavor for its introduction to local dishes like breadfruit-cheddar soufflé and the restaurant's signature specialties like fresh lobster with grapefruit butter and conch stuffing. A surprisingly good selection of wines, including Napa's Silver Oak, complement the evening and make you realize, as you linger over your table, that you really are staying somewhere unbelievably special.

ROOMS

The fifteen different guest lodgings range from separate wooden cottages to a seventeenth-century stone building to a replica manor house. Each room was individually decorated by Maureen, who favors a traditional Caribbean décor, which she accents with curio cabinets filled with colorful knickknacks and paintings by local artists. When the Lupinaccis first decided to expand, they needed to fill the rooms with furniture, fast. They took the few precious antiques from the great house and their former home in Barbardos, like their original Regency-style dining room table and heirloom canopy bed, to local carpenters to have them copied and to teach them the signature design and style so they could adorn the property in a set period style. Modest yet fresh and clean, the deluxe cottages are my favorite category of cottages. Although they're smaller and less well-appointed than the luxury cottages (whose added luxury is a television with VCR), their tighter dimensions create a cozy environment and repurpose the cottages to what they're really for— sleeping. All of the cottages feature louvered windows, French doors, pitched ceilings with ceiling fans, and verandas decorated with a hammock or wicker chairs. Twin Gables, a deluxe cottage, is my first pick. Painted a sunny yellow and having a row of matching allamanda flowers, the cottage feels cheerful and inherently welcoming. Overlooking the garden pool and devoid of any sea view, the charm is in the faded toile canopy bed and polished floors that give it the unique style of an English bungalow,

both transporting and romantic. The small foyer doubles as a sitting room, with an antique mahogany settee and corner desk, though most of the lounging space is on the screened back porch, a nice spot to read, even at dusk when the bugs appear. My next choice would be Pasture House, a luxury cottage whose secluded location and unassuming gray-shingled façade lend it a do-not-disturb quality that ensures privacy. (For those not into mingling, this is the top choice.) For larger groups who still want the historically styled lodgings but with a bit more privacy, there is the three-bedroom yellow Manor House and the newer four-bedroom villa Mango. A complete replica of a seventeenth-century Nevis manor house, the two-story Manor House is better for those who want to experience the property's funky, historic style. Located higher up on the hill than the great house, the latticed-covered house has its own private garden, kitchen, and ceramic-tiled pool. The elevated position offers sweeping views of the property, historic Gingerland, and the sparkling sea. The arched living room and spacious dining room (seating ten) open out to the veranda while the upper-level master bedrooms have muslin-draped canopy beds and sets of French doors that permit the cool evening breeze and morning sunlight to fill the rooms. More recently, the Lupinaccis have begun to build luxury villas, still in the tradition of the Nevisian house, with porches and shingles, though with custom designs as per each owner's desires.

ABOVE   *The colonial-style dining room that seems more for show than actual use.*

OPPOSITE PAGE   *The classic English bar, complete with brass railing.*

FIREFLY PLANTATION *BEQUIA*
AND FIREFLY *MUSTIQUE*

*L*ike most sisters who are close in age, these petite Grenadine Island properties, separated by less than eleven miles of sea, are total contrasts of one another. Conceived by the same owner, Elizabeth Clayton, the two- , four- , and five-bedroom Firefly properties, one on Mustique, the other on Bequia, offset each other perfectly. Where one is gussied up and social by nature, the other is relaxed and rooted in its surroundings. Combined, the two provide the ideal island vacation that satisfies both of a holiday's core desires—to let loose and live more extravagantly than normal and to unwind and rejuvenate. Luckily, the owner agrees and has instilled attractive packages offering complimentary air or boat transport between the two islands. I highly recommend going by boat charter—it's an easy, pleasant sail and you can even hang a line off the back and try to catch dinner! Of course, those suited to only one of those intentions can rest assured that both properties feature Firefly's characteristic luxury-minded details.

OPPOSITE PAGE   *Firefly Mustique's famous watering hole.*

ABOVE   *The iron signage of Firefly Mustique.*

FIREFLY PLANTATION

BEQUIA

Situated in the quiet, residential areas of Industry Beach and Spring Bay, on the grounds of a working plantation, Firefly Plantation Bequia is as remote as it can get. Heralded for its sleepy, vintage Caribbean nature, the six-square-mile island of Bequia is ideal for those who simply want to unplug and soak up the white, sandy beaches, bathtub-temperature waters, and tropical flora and

fauna. On Bequia boats are still built by hand, the "coconut telegraph" (the local gossip line) is remarkably strong, and the locals are friendly. The main port, Port Elizabeth, is chockablock with salty sailors while the Swedish appear to be the foreign majority. But everyone on the island agrees that the slow pace on Bequia is the preferred way to live.

Built on the foundation of an eighteenth-century West Indian homestead, the thirty-acre Firefly Plantation, formerly known as Spring Plantation, remains a working farm with orchards full of grapefruit, breadfruit, guava, mangoes, and over a hundred banana trees. The quaint herb garden is a shared passion of the property manager, Anita, and the head gardener, Keith, both of whom will eagerly point out its contents or hail its usage in the restaurant's dishes. The traditional foundation of the property, including a 250-year-old sugar mill and indigo-processing plant, gives the exterior instant character. Climbing up the driveway to the cut-stone walls of Firefly's main building and passing the fields of towering coconut groves to the right, maybe even spying a stray cow from the neighboring pasture, is perhaps the most authentic Caribbean arrival today. Affable hosts from South Africa, Anita, and her husband, François, will greet you

with hugs and flustering exclamations over your arrival (Anita and François treat each arrival like a long-lost houseguest) while barman Rodney mixes up one of Firefly's signature rum punches. Take heed, both Rodney's fruity concoctions and witty banter is intoxicating, leading to next-day headaches and midafternoon splurges. Fortunately the sobering sea is just a five-minute walk down the hill and virtually uninhabited, making your bathing suit judiciously optional. The pavilion-style main room with stone floors and a wooden frame is the hub of activity. The central stool-studded bar, casual lounge area with orange-cushioned sofas, and relaxed dining area with simple square tables all share the same long space, though given the hotel's low guest maximum (sixteen) and off-the-beaten-track location, it's never loud and rarely occupied. The casual, funky décor, including polished turtle shells, locally made sculptures, and glass globe lanterns, immediately translates the laid-back, come-as-you-are vibe of the property. At the front edge of the room is a row of plantation chairs, set into pairs, overlooking the cut-stone deck of the freshwater pool sparkling underneath the curvy coconut groves. For those who love coconuts, Firefly Plantation Bequia's fresh, homemade coconut cream

is a godsend, making you swear off the canned stuff forever.

The view is remarkably unspoiled, devoid of any surrounding development other than the few neighboring residences tucked higher up in the hills. The working plantation is the forefront of the property and tours are always available and well worth the experience (particularly when Keith has you tasting the tangy, indigenous fruits). There's a weather-beaten tennis court just down the hill and walking (or jogging) the mile-and-a-half coastal route past grazing goats to the modest turtle sanctuary provides intimate glimpses into the area's bucolic lifestyle. Taking a picnic down to the beach or strolling to the next bay and trying out the relaxed beach bar's catch of the day feels like modern pleasure for a castaway. A rental car is a good idea if you want to scoot into the main port town or around to various beaches, bars, and restaurants at your own leisure; otherwise, taxis are readily available including water taxis from Port Elizabeth. For a truly hidden stay in a lesser-known part of the Caribbean, where peace and quiet are not just advertised but sincerely inescapable, Firefly Plantation Bequia is the infallible choice.

ROOMS

The four guest rooms at Firefly Plantation Bequia are the most detailed interiors of the property. As the rooms are housed in a separate, contemporary structure just up the hill, getting to them involves a bit of a hike and multiple steps, and although tiki torches light the way at

PREVIOUS PAGE *Firefly's brand new guestrooms with designer linens introduce a new luxury standard on Bequia.*

ABOVE, FROM LEFT TO RIGHT *Coconuts ready to be turned into delicious cream for desserts, drinks, and even bath oils; the plantation's homemade fruit preserves on display.*

OPPOSITE PAGE *The signature cut-stone stairs leading down to the pool.*

night, it's not recommended for the weary. The four rooms are stacked on top of one another, two on the bottom and two on top. The upper-level suites are the obvious preference for their superior views and large balconies looking out to the sea. However, the rooms on the first floor are slightly longer and have one fewer set of stairs to climb at the end of the evening. Either way, you'll be guaranteed a good night's sleep because all four rooms feature brand-new king-size four-poster beds with white Sferra bedding. Bose iPod docks with pre-programmed iPods are ready and waiting (the sailing playlist is my favorite) while walk-in closets include stocked minibars and silk sarongs on hangers. Each room's cut-stone walls and sleek, dark furniture create an element of austerity; however, once you've tucked yourself into the soft sheets, untied the muslin netting around the bed, and left the sliding doors to the balcony open to the trade winds, the romance of the rooms is clear. The

absence of a television is also wonderfully soothing. If the open doors tend to invite the uninvited, rest assured the rooms have both ceiling fans and air-conditioning. The minimal embellishments include locally made wall-mounted iron-work sculptures, plantation-style teak chairs, and a straw basket filled with striped towels and snorkel gear left at the entryway. The bathrooms, however, are a master of design and detail with spacious, white-tiled walk-in showers with pebbled floors, each having sliding glass doors that open onto a balcony, plus a generous selection of Firefly's own tropically scented shampoos. Surprisingly, the guest rooms' lack of customary island colors and local watercolor prints feels wholly welcome after a day out and about in Bequia. The rooms' high quality, not to mention the overall upgrade from what's otherwise available on the island, allows them to stand out as the top choice for the choosy traveler who appreciates the finer things whenever available.

CLOCKWISE FROM TOP LEFT   *Walk-in pebbled-floor showers in the spacious guest bathrooms; a cushioned, orange sectional sets the casual tone of the lounge and restaurant area; the canopy mosquito netting ensures the feel of an island romance; Firefly's in-room welcome basket comes complete with snorkel gear and sarongs.*

The plantation's fertile surroundings.

FIREFLY

MUSTIQUE

World-renowned for its exclusivity, the private island of Mustique is the finely groomed, sophisticated Grenadine. The island was once the private retreat of Lord Glenconner (the Honorable Colin Tennant), and its population originally grew only through personal invitation from Tennant. His friends, like HRH Princess Margaret, were given land upon which to build their own villas. Soon after, friends were inviting friends (though Tennant's opinion was always consulted, if not required) and by 1989 the island transformed from a family estate into a community-managed, privately held company. Today, it is touted as one of the most rarefied playgrounds of the superwealthy, known for its massive villas, white sandy beaches (Macaroni Beach is easily one of the prettiest in the Caribbean), and bold-name guests.

The five-room Firefly buzzes in the center of it all as one of only two popular watering holes on island (the other is the waterfront Basil's Bar). Firefly, along with Basil's, are the only two properties that exist outside of the Mustique Company's domain and are thus able to operate as private businesses, catering to the island's well-heeled crowd, oftentimes late into the evening. The fifteen-year old Firefly is lauded as the bar to see and be seen in—its baby grand piano has been rumored to have more than a few famous fingers tickle its ivories. Built high into the hillside just above the island's small harbor, Firefly's hilltop location offers sweeping views of the western coast of the island, the sea, and the island of Canouan in the distance. The square-shaped mahogany bar backs up to the view, flanked on either side by wood-framed panoramas, while the elegantly carved bar seats are affixed with brass plaques featuring names of friends, past guests, and of course, the legendary owner, Stan Clayton, whose seat needs no identifying, given that it's usually filled by the character himself. At sunset, the bar's intimate gazebo-like space is bathed in pink light and every barstool and seat has a front-row view. If you find it's too packed, take your drink down to the terraced stone pool, recently refurbished with lights, and enjoy the view from the hammock or thatched-roof daybed. The pool area's white gazebo is a secluded spot under lush palms, perfect for private dining or a shaded lunch, yet equipped with a telephone that rings up to the bar, ensuring drinks and food are never far away. The small size of Firefly Mustique and its relative quiet during the day keeps the exclusivity of the property at an all-time high. The casual, terrace dining room with red-tile floor and gabled wood ceilings serves only guests at breakfast—order a tropical smoothie. Parked in a row outside the front entrance are the complimentary red-and-white electric carts—mules, as they're known locally—with trunk space in the back for the hotel's delicious, packed beach picnics and emblazoned with "Firefly" on the side.

ROOMS

All five rooms at Firefly Mustique are decorated in the classic English style of owner Elizabeth Clayton. Gauzy white curtains, pale tiled floors, plantation-style hardwood furnishings, and charming details like backgammon boards and silk sarongs in the closet are all signatures of Elizabeth's fastidious design. Three of Firefly's rooms lie right beneath the popular bar, which can be a nuisance for those who came for peace and quiet but on the flip side, can be one of the best locations in town. Nevertheless, each of the rooms has been recently outfitted with double-glazed mahogany sliding doors for better noise insulation, ensuring a good night's sleep at whatever hour you desire. Accessed by a tight spiral staircase in the center of the bar's floor (for some it might as well be a fireman's pole), the three rooms beneath the bar have a clubby appeal to them. My favorite room, Pineapple, is right underneath the bar, but its breezy, sophisticated tropical décor and crystal-clear sea views overrode my initial discomfort. The largest of the lower three rooms, Pineapple features an alcove studio shape that allows for a small sitting area with plantation-style chairs, pineapple prints, and a Louis XV–style chaise. Two floor-length picture windows (also double-glazed), complete with billowing white curtains, frame the view though usually the windows are shut at night for the air-conditioning because the room can get hot. A new king-size bed with fine Italian linens faces out to the view yet lies just two feet from the room's exotic, freestanding shower constructed entirely

PREVIOUS PAGES   *Firefly Mustique's terraced pool overlooking the island's harbor.*

OPPOSITE PAGE   *Royal Palm, one of the more secluded guest rooms at Firefly Mustique.*

ABOVE   *Lace-trimmed cream linens bring Old World charm to the guest rooms.*

of sea pebbles. Not for the bashful, the circular, exposed shower provides a sensual element to the otherwise classically styled room. If you are a light sleeper or require a bit more space and privacy, the remaining two suites located down the hill are the wise option. Both Royal Palm and Seashell have been recently upgraded with extended patios and new

bathrooms. Royal Palm, the more popular of the two and the most secluded room in the hotel, also has new, pale limestone flooring that extends out onto the patio, giving the room a brighter, airy look despite its tucked-away location. Both Elizabeth and Stan offer plenty of suggestions for how to best appreciate the island—from nature

walks to secluded beach picnics—and their fifteen years on the island grant them expert status. Although staying at Firefly Mustique may feel a bit like a watered-down version of the Mustique experience, given Firefly's character and position as the favored hangout, you're bound to feel right in the heart of the action.

ABOVE, FROM LEFT TO RIGHT *A feminine, old-fashioned appeal abounds in the guest room; the bar's prime seating, come sunset.*

Plantation chairs lend a patrician feel to the guest room.

AURORA

MUSTIQUE

*P*ulling up to the villa Aurora's modest, typically Caribbean exterior may feel a tad underwhelming after the mansion-studded drive from Mustique's airport. However, rest assured that as a guest of Aurora, you are exactly where you want to be to appreciate the elevated level of interior décor typical of Mustique. Perhaps purposely, the four-bedroom villa, which includes an older,

separate one-bedroom cottage, stuns its guests right upon entry. Just a few steps up from the narrow driveway, Aurora's flattened perch atop a hill presents surprisingly sweeping views out to the south and east, overlooking the famous Macaroni Beach. The straightforward, L shape of the villa appears simple yet graceful around a series of pools that diminish in size, and is complemented by arched doorways and a stand-alone dining gazebo. Despite the remarkable fluidity of the villa's architecture, once the guest glimpses the elegant medley of furnishings and objets d'art in the front sitting room, the focus of the house quickly turns inward.

Owner Mark Cecil commands an eye for design and the villa's richly appointed front room is his apparent pièce de résistance. Mark's classic, refined taste (colonial English) and fondness for fine collectibles is on full display in this veritable antiques showroom. Hanging front and center on the far wall of the room is a giant mirror that was converted from a skylight of a Victorian school, flanked on either side by ten-foot tall, eighteenth-century Piranesi prints. Beneath the mirror is a simple mahogany console table, although hardly simply adorned—its top is littered with Chinese porcelain, nineteenth-century

ivory and ebony whale sculptures from a Natural History Museum in England, and Indonesian mother-of-pearl boxes. The square room features tall, gabled ceilings, complete with exposed cupola and fan to keep the room nice and cool. Custom touches include aged, hand-painted signs bearing the names of surrounding islands atop the room's seven sets of French doors. Two opposing Regency mahogany settees are stuffed with China Seas Nitik II fabric pillows in blues and beiges to encourage a sense of comfort amid the opulence, while an iron lantern chandelier gives the room a sense of individual, if not distinctly original, character. More antique and original pieces include a pair of Regency console tables set into mirrored alcoves and two large circular mirrors with reptile-skin frames brought back from South Africa. Despite the formality of some of the pieces in the room, the front console table is anchored with coral sculptures and a large collection of polished conch shells to remind the viewer that yes, you are still on an island.

Finished in 2003, Aurora took just two years to build, which is fast for a new building all the way down in the Grenadines (but then Mustique does have its own private construction company). Mark commemorates all those

who were involved in a framed photograph hanging in the bathroom off the pool. The multilevel pool makes its own style statement, with three rectangular pools that offer various options for to cool off or just float luxuriously. Surrounded by lounge chairs and a faded teak daybed, the pool terrace is an easy spot to lose your afternoon. Just above the pool, up a garden stone staircase, is a bona fide pirate's lookout spot with a small, seventeenth-century ruin. There, Mark wisely created a small patio with a bench because the views of the sunset are equally as genuine. Although the grounds at Aurora are admittedly tight, fortunately there are no neighbors within sight and the landscaping is colorfully designed, keeping the villa's hideaway feeling firmly intact. Mark sought to create a hamlet he hoped would sustain his artful style yet appease guests all the same. Despite its relatively small size, the villa features all the necessary luxury amenities to ensure it competes with other island rentals including a media room, gourmet kitchen, Wi-Fi, and an excellent chef, Tyrone, whose mahi-mahi is legendary. The generous veranda off the sitting room is yet another spot to repose amid stylish furnishings while soaking in the panoramic sea view. Teak benches and plantation-style chairs rest atop a sisal area rug while potted palms and handsome pineapple sconces on the outside wall enhance the tropical feel. Meals are served either on the veranda or in the whitewashed dining gazebo. Dwayne, the loyal butler, enjoys mixing his version of a Bloody Mary (he wouldn't divulge his recipe) or a tangy rum punch,

PREVIOUS PAGE   *The collector's showcase—Aurora's living room.*

BELOW, FROM TOP TO BOTTOM   *Twin Regency tables frame the main entry into the living room; Aurora's whitewashed dining gazebo.*

OPPOSITE PAGE   *The villa's secluded location on Mustique.*

while the terrier housedog, Reggie, will happily join you for jogs around the island's hilly terrain.

In typical antique-collector fashion, the rooms in the villa seem to be bursting at the seams with interesting pieces and valuable curios. In an island environment where interiors are often left to minimalism, Aurora's complex décor is a wonderful distinction.

ROOMS

The three bedrooms in the main house of Aurora all face out towards Macaroni Beach and have marble bathrooms, pebbled-floor showers, and private terraces. The master bedroom features a massive bathroom/dressing room, although it is oddly situated between the bedroom and the entryway, meaning one must walk through it to access the bedroom. The room is well proportioned though with a white nineteenth-century French Provençal four-poster bed staring out toward the sea and an attractive Goyard chest. The mood is determinedly fresh and airy. Alongside the master is a twin canopy-bed room with more whitewashed Provençal-style French furniture that Mark found in flea markets. The twin room shares the same airiness as the master and is ideal for children. Jasmine, the one-bedroom cottage, with its shabby-chic décor and own kitchen and separate entrance, suits nannies or older children perfectly. Although given the property's exceptional collection of vintage pieces and island artifacts, there was never any contest: my preferred room at Aurora is also the smallest. The third bedroom lies off to the right with a private entrance off the pool and differs

greatly in design and character from the white-walled front rooms. Its detailed décor is more in keeping with the drawing room. Decorated in a pronounced eighteenth-century, island colonial style, the room's caramel-colored walls, framed eighteenth- and nineteenth-century antique maps of Mustique and the Grenadines and two vintage Goyard steamer trunks set a handsome, rugged tone, which is furthered by polished wood floors and eclectic pieces like an apothecary chest and massive seventeenth-century Spanish chest. As if a traveler has come to rest here, the room is a stage set with exotic finds—a large, handmade bowl of ostrich eggs from Africa, carved whalebones and ivory from Ceylon. Perhaps the most signature element though is the polished leatherback turtle shell emblazoned with the royal insignia of St. Vincent in painted gold. The commemorative shell comes from a turtle that was eaten by the crew of the HMS St. Vincent, who were stuck at sea for several weeks. The turtle is said to have saved their lives. It's also Mark's most prized piece in the entire treasure-filled villa. Femininity can also be found in the room through the nineteenth-century Anglo-Indian canopy bed and its delicately embroidered linen curtains and ornately carved headboard. The adjoining bathroom is comfortably spacious with double vanities and a walk-in pebbled-floor shower. The room's coral-tile terrace features two teak lawn chairs and a daybed and looks out over Macaroni Beach. Leave the curtains open at night so that the first sight you have in the morning is the sliding doors framing the brilliant Caribbean sunrise.

ABOVE, FROM LEFT TO RIGHT *The carved bed of the explorer's guest room; the commemorative turtle shell of* HMS St. Vincent *in the guest room.*

OPPOSITE PAGE *Mahogany furnishings on the covered veranda.*

YEMANJÁ

MUSTIQUE

Yemanjá's enormous *palapa*, a Mexican thatched roof-pavilion designed by Manolo Mestre, announces the Mustique villa's prominence with steadfast confidence—even defiant confidence. Climbing up the palm-fringed driveway, winding past the tennis court (whose sweeping ocean views claim frequent double faults) and the stone guest cottage, Bahia, with its own sleek, infinity lap pool, is truly breathtaking, in that you must remind yourself to exhale. Equal parts awe-inspiring and intimidating, the sprawling hilltop property was constructed to house the owner's large extended family, including over twenty grandchildren. To call Yemanjá a compound would denigrate its elegant pedigree while labeling it a villa seems an awkward underestimation. Rather, Yemanjá's sophisticated décor, exemplary craftsmanship, and customized details recall those of a refined superyacht. With three separate buildings, multiple pools, including a shallow wading pool for toddlers, and at least five dining areas in the main house, Yemanjá is perhaps the most exquisitely designed multi-generational villa in the Caribbean. Of course, the sharp eye and elegant style of the owner, a former proprietor of a Brazilian fine linen and children's clothing line, are largely accountable. Immaculately conceived, every corner of every room, particularly the guest rooms, demonstrates a distinct and thoughtful design aesthetic. Unlike properties in which rooms are disproportionally decorated according to size, or worse, their view, at Yemanjá every single tabletop, upholstered furnishing and window treatment showcases interior design prowess. Whether it's the exotic, handcrafted furnishings imported from the far reaches of South America and Africa, or the delicate embroidered bed linens from the owner's native Brazil, or even the shell strung shower curtains, Yemanjá's superlative décor is impressively consistent.

Befitting its glamorous proportions, the entrance to Yemanjá's main building begins with a regal, curved staircase leading up from the driveway. The stonewalled foyer, however, is graciously modest with a subtle, pebbled floor design, an antique wood table, and a back wall open to frame the initial view of Yemanjá's lush interior gardens. Hanging above the table is a gold-toned painting of the ethereal Yemanjá, the Brazilian goddess of the sea, who is said to protect all those who enter. A cut-stone path leads out from the entryway into the grass yard and then breaks off into tentacles toward the various wings and outdoor spaces of the main house. At the path's heart is a custom-made pebble mosaic featuring a ring of five waves meant to represent the owners' five daughters. The design is in the property's insignia and can be found monogrammed on towels, robes, and toiletries throughout the house, making the comparison to a yacht even more appropriate. Given Yemanjá's high-quality interior design, the property risks being overwhelmingly perfect. Fortunately, the Latin-style architecture and flowing indoor-outdoor layout counter that impression with soothing curved edges, whimsical stone paths through the water, and several lounge spots, such as the mesmerizing tree sofa in the *palapa*, which is to soak in the expansive views. Decorated with the honed patience of a true designer, the one-of-a-kind furnishings at Yemanjá will delight any collector and include the canoe-shaped dining table behind the *palapa* made from railroad ties from South Africa and the mahogany coffee table found in France. Fellow enthusiasts will note showpieces from designers such Baker Furniture (planters chairs in the *palapa*), Oggetti in Miami (tub chairs in *palapa*), and accessories from Palacek and The Phillips Collection. However, it's the handcrafted coconut and bamboo cabinets in the media room done by Industrias Exporenso in Bogotá and coconut shell trim on the floor length-curtains that showcase the considerable attention paid to every detail.

What makes Yemanjá even more spectacular is its ability to be both a casual, family retreat during the day and a sophisticated backdrop for cocktail hour and lavish dinner parties as the light fades. Guests can go from draping themselves across the Hermès-blanketed daybed under the *palapa,* to claiming one of the barstools, swirling a crystal-encased rum concoction from Pairson, whose eleven years of Brazilian and Italian guests have given him a generous hand. Despite the relaxation and seclusion afforded on property, I would still recommend packing your better outfits—not only is it Mustique, but Yemanjá's fine fabrics (Lee Jofa, China Seas, Brunschwig and Fils, Quadrille and trimmings from M and J) will certainly expose a lesser-made frock.

Truly, no desire or request is out of reach or over-the-top when you're a guest at Yemanjá, though, admirably, the atmosphere does little to suggest prima-donna-type behavior. If anything, the laid-back nature of the staff and the absence of today's super-luxe amenities (private screening room, private gym) keep the property rooted in its purpose of indulging its guests with space, views, and sophisticated interiors. With a staff of sixteen, including three gardeners, Yemanjá is constantly being polished and nurtured, and thus, so are the guests. Meals are served with printed menus at dinner (the owner's decree) and there is a binder for guests to view past menus to use as guides when designing their own. The fluffy cheese soufflé at lunch with home-brewed iced tea followed by a lobster salad was perhaps the most delicious lunch I had in the Caribbean. One of the daily pastimes at Yemanjá is deciding where to dine. With five separate eating alcoves, the decision can feel almost weighty. I recommend switching it up every day to try all the spots until, that is, you've decided your favorite for each time of day. I do, also, highly suggest hosting a dinner party while in residence at Yemanjá. The oval dining room table, seating twenty-two and located on a level below the pool, offers a fabulous opportunity to showcase Yemanjá's impressive collection of china and tableware while simultaneously allowing for a lively evening tucked into the hill. The chef's tangy curries with fresh coconut shavings are the ideal complement to the festivities, or for something

more casual, take advantage of the barbecue and pizza oven and request a variety of fresh flatbreads. Surrounded by such refined luxury, it would be a downright shame to waste it with faux prudence. Instead, host an elegant dinner party and relish being the temporary hostess of one of the most cultivated properties in the Caribbean.

ROOMS

Split into three separate structures, the guest rooms at Yemanjá are designed to afford privacy, appease children, and envelop guests in sophisticated, comfortable décor. Boasting eight bedrooms in total, not including the children's cottages (one for girls, the other for boys), Yemanjá has plenty of space for the multi-generational family reunion or a shared family vacation. The main house features five bedrooms. My favorite, aside from the elegant, whitewashed master bedroom, is Acarajé. The pale blue design on the coverlet on the four-poster mahogany bed had me at first glance. The thick raffia rug, bamboo desk from Minas Gerais in Brazil, and antique trunk imported from a shop in Connecticut all fall into place, belying the tremendous effort and sourcing that brought them together. The master bedroom is towards the back of the main house and done all in pale creams, beiges, and whites, with exotic prints of African dancers inspired by Carybé. The four-poster bamboo bed with palm fringe copper tops is particularly alluring with rows of plump-pressed pillows and a tufted headboard. I imagine mornings spent lounging with coffee and a book breaking

only to gaze out the French doors to the glistening sea. The children's bunkhouses, located alongside the main house, are a Neverland-fantasy realized with murals on the walls and play areas between each bunkroom. There's even a trampoline in the adjacent yard and extra space for nannies. Bahia, the guest cottage, has three bedrooms and is ideal for those needing a bit of distance from the main house and its neighboring children's quarters. Self-sufficient, the cottage has its own mini *palapa*, (*palapita*), lap pool, living room, and kitchen. The upstairs bedroom, Jangada (all the rooms are named after Brazilian fruits and delicacies), is my favorite, with its four-poster bamboo bed made by Paul Briger in San Miguel de Allende, shell-trimmed bed curtains and cheerful butter-yellow palette. All the guest rooms of Yemanjá feature delicate embroidered bed linens, ironed to perfection, that add a level of refinement rarely found in the Caribbean. The cottage's back bedroom has twin beds, making it ideal for single guests or kids who've outgrown the bunk beds of the children's cottages. The bottom bedroom, or suite as they all appear to be, opens out to the long grassy lawn and the inviting infinity pool. Its blue-and-white fabrics with polka-dot patterns make it an instant crowd-pleaser while the spacious window seat mitigates rainy days with coziness.

Whichever guest room you claim, you can rest assured the linens will be exquisite, the furnishings distinctly paired, and the experience wonderfully privileged.

PREVIOUS PAGES   *Yemanjá's infinity pool and eminent Palapa.*

ABOVE, FROM LEFT TO RIGHT   *The charming guest cottage,*
Bahia; quirky iron palm tops accent the Bamboo bed in the Master bedroom.

OPPOSITE PAGE   *The villa's stunning view, over the pool, of the island's beloved Macaroni Beach.*

ABOVE   *Designer furnishings fit for a* palapa.

CLOCKWISE FROM TOP LEFT   *Brazilian prints adorn the walls while decorative pillows confirm the detailed interior design; embroidered linens on the bed in Acarajé; the foyer where the portrait of Yemanjá hangs and thus is viewed upon entry; a tempting reading corner in Acarajé.*

OPPOSITE PAGE   *Shell-trimmed bed curtains offer textured glamour in a guest room in Bahia.*

COTTON HOUSE

MUSTIQUE

One of two hotels on an island dominated by villas and the fortunate regulars who inhabit them, Mustique's Cotton House provides access to the exclusive enclave without the weeklong commitment. Fortunately, its position as the social hub of the island and formal, elegant appearance disavow it from any stigma of inferiority. The twenty rooms and suites, including a separate two-bedroom cottage, are spread around the thirteen-acre property in either traditional coral stone buildings or more contemporary Caribbean-style cement structures with gingerbread trim and wraparound verandas. The manicured grounds, with their lily ponds and cut-stone paths that lead past a seventeenth-century windmill, lend an Old World quality. The roundabout driveway appears to be eternally waiting for a horse-drawn carriage. The main house, known as the Cotton House, features a wraparound porch filled with cushioned wicker lounge chairs and sofas, plus weatherworn white Adirondack chairs, which continue the mood of timeless grace. In one corner is the veranda dining area that serves all three meals, including an Italian-inspired evening menu. (The breaded veal chops and green salad are simple yet well prepared.) The veranda and spacious interior of the main house play host to a weekly wine tasting and cocktail party to which all of the guests from the entire island are invited. The party, usually held on Tuesdays, can be a veritable collection of who's who, including members of the Royal Family and the occasional rock star and fashion icon. A polished baby grand piano holds court in one corner of the long, open room while a large mahogany bar anchors the back wall. A handful of dark teak seating areas with Moroccan-inspired pillows and carved lanterns give the room a particular non-Caribbean sensibility, while the light-colored, vaulted ceilings and collection of shell-adorned furnishings keep it from feeling too heavy. The great room is also where the informal check-in is held. Once the house lemonade punches are distributed, arriving guests, the guests are seated either on the veranda or on one of the many couches while the manager fetches the necessary papers. The process is an orchestrated introduction to the Cotton House's demonstrably laid-back (presuming all their guests possess suitable manners) and peaceful atmosphere.

The property's spa and gym, located just a hundred or so yards from the Cotton House, is an exemplar of plantation-style architecture. The two-story stone building has, on the second floor, a covered veranda supported by thick stone columns. The spa's treatment rooms are right off the veranda with windows that let in the sea breeze and offer views toward the sea. The small gym, just below the spa, has large French doors looking out across the grassy field toward the house's restored eighteenth-century stone buildings. There's a recommended jog around the Cotton House's property that, if you want, can also take you back along the beach, offering fantastic peeks into some jaw-dropping beachfront mansions, including Tommy Hilfiger's Palm Beach-style home. A small, signature boutique with top-name designers and enviable, refined beachwear sits alongside the spa entrance—making it difficult, for even the most disciplined, to avoid. Alas, after just half a day at the Cotton House (and on Mustique in general), splurging feels almost obligatory. The neighboring Beach Café is another hotspot for the local community to gather, particularly for the weekly beach barbecues following the revered outdoor movie nights, where films are projected on a screen just outside the spa and gym building. The evening is a chance for villa residents and guests of the hotel to mingle and one of the few times you're guaranteed to see some of the more private Mustique residents out and about. Unlike other enclaves of the rich and famous, the Cotton House is wonderfully unassuming, void of pretension, and rooted in providing guests a sophisticated yet comfortable backdrop to enjoy themselves—no matter who they are.

ROOMS

Given that the Cotton House, as a hotel, is the anomaly on Mustique, the property best serves short stays or travelers who may crave some autonomy from friends staying in a villa. In order to choose the appropriate accommodation, it's important to consider the number in the group and its dynamic; some rooms offer greater privacy, along with ameni-

PREVIOUS PAGE   *Wonderfully secluded—the Cotton House spa and gym area.*

OPPOSITE PAGE   *Assured quietude at the Cotton House pool.*

ABOVE   *Lush goose down pillows and drawn mosquito netting on the guest beds at the Cotton House.*

ties that may seem unnecessary to some and vital to others. The oceanfront cottages offer the most inspiring beach-themed interiors with treated wood furnishings, limestone floors, and the most intimate sea views. They also have square-shaped dip pools, though given the cottages' close proximity to the warm Caribbean waters, these seem unnecessary to me. The two-bedroom cottages share similarly styled interiors and amenities like private dip pools, but they are a bit more secluded and spacious given their distance from the shared beach and indoor-outdoor layout, making them a better option should you wish to entertain. Although if it's entertaining that you're really after, then I would search the Mustique Island listings for a

private villa and full staff. The Cotton House's duplex suites, situated up on the hill, farther away from the main house and the beach, are ideal for couples with small children. Maddox, a yellow duplex suite with contemporary bamboo furnishings, bright aqua blue and white walls, and a large, private pool, feels the most secluded of its category, despite its upside-down design (the bedroom is on the floor below the sitting rooms). Nevertheless, the muslin-covered four-poster bed in the ground-level master bedroom offers one of the best night's sleep in the Caribbean, with crisp yet soft sheets, just the right fluff in the pillows, and delectable quiet save for the ceiling fan. Of all seventeen guest rooms, my favorites are those in the stone bell-tower-like struc-

ture, called the Coutinot House. Located as close to the beach as possible and facing west, the rooms' private terraces are just the spot to appreciate a private cocktail at sunset. The rooms' unfussy white wicker furniture and polished wood floors appear wholly Caribbean, but with an eye toward classic appointment and simple comforts. The beds are similar to those in the duplex suites, though the rooms are smaller. But surrounded by frayed palms that whisper in the breeze and undisturbed views of the sea's aquamarine glory, all you need is the coziness of the room and the veranda.

CLOCKWISE FROM TOP LEFT   *Cocktail hour on the wraparound porch at the Cotton House; the artful décor in the main lounge; the warm glow of the Cotton House at dusk; a shell-shaped foot bath on the beach.*

The colonial-style entrance to the beachfront rooms.

THE HORNED DORSET PRIMAVERA

PUERTO RICO

After a (necessary) phone call for directions, the gray wooden gates of the Horned Dorset Primavera resort appear like a mirage against Rincón's Route 429's iron–and–concrete-laden dwellings. The doors open to reveal a combed gravel driveway and the whitewashed façade of the resort's garden suites. The reception area is housed in a low-slung cottage with hacienda-style red-tile roofing and doubles as the small gift shop and lone wireless Internet area. Ramón, the eager voice from the phone call, greets you with a smile and offers to unload the car and deliver the luggage to your room. The doubts that had accrued along the drive from the airport begin to dissipate.

The architecture of the twenty-two-year-old Horned Dorset Primavera resort can be most simply described as Spanish colonial (mahogany shutter windows, curved iron balconies) meets Caribbean practicality (concrete and white walls). The eight-acre hillside property sits right on the beach and faces southwest, allowing for a constant soundtrack of crashing waves and enviable sunsets. Thick tropical vegetation and chirping birdsong surround the property while artful landscaping, including bushes of bougainvillea, frangipani, and allamanda strike a refined and elegant tone. The property features a total of three pools. The center infinity pool, despite being the smallest of the three, tends to see the most action, given its attractive blue-and–white-striped lounge chairs and alluring view out to the calm waters of the Mona Passage. The beach, despite being somewhat narrow, is a soothing spot to spend the top sunning hours. The bright yellow umbrellas, minimal guests, and wading-friendly water, not to mention the full beach service, offer a serene experience.

Given that the property is a member of the Relais & Châteaux hotel group, the on-site restaurant, Aaron, presents a gourmet menu that attracts outside diners—though never enough to impede guests' plans. Located on the second floor of the two-story plantation-style house, complete with an imperial staircase, the restaurant evokes Old World sophistication with checkerboard marble floors, red-shaded chandeliers, and starched white tablecloths. However, the best seat in the house is found inside the restaurant's small side alcove on the left, found through a narrow archway framed by stained-glass window panels. Inside, the walls are painted in a trompe l'oeil style with surrealistic murals of eclectic nature scenes, including the artist's vision of a horned dorset (it looks like a white elk), and a former waiter immortalized as Cupid, creating a romantic, candlelit ambience. The six tables feature flickering votives and handsome high-back chairs that are locally made reproductions of the Spanish Isabella chair. The vintage glass-dome chandelier and brass sconces were brought in by a New York antiques dealer while the corner mahogany-shut-tered windows give the room a tucked-in, nautical feel. Continental cuisine mixed with occasional Caribbean flair (such as mahi-mahi with pineapple salsa or plantain-stuffed pork loin) is offered alongside an extensive wine list, which includes many more options than other Caribbean restaurants, given Puerto Rico's connection to the U.S. The daily dessert soufflé (mine was guava) is worth ordering, with warm guava-and-lemon crème anglaise poured on top. The restaurant's menu is simple enough that eating there every night of your stay is hardly a chore—particularly since the local options are not recommended for anything beyond burgers at lunch.

The resort's three other dining areas are used exclusively for breakfast and lunch, with the exception of the Blue Room, which can be reserved for private functions. The veranda restaurant, is comprised of an open porch area divided between rattan couches adorned with attractive elephant-print pillows and white-clothed tables. The delightfully small beachside patio, with room for only seven or eight tables, is my favorite for breakfast, given its front-row seating along the beach and neighboring massive seagrape tree, which keeps it comfortably cool. Every night cocktails and light tapas are served at 6:00 p.m. on the ocean side of the veranda. Drinks are poured at the antique carved wooden bar tucked into the back wall of the tiny library. Pedro, the shy bartender, will deliver your drink to the plush yellow-and-white-striped cushioned chairs along the terrace's ocean-side railing. From there, the romantic pink light of the sunset is dramatically unveiled. Note

PREVIOUS PAGES *Iconic yellow umbrellas on the beach at Horned Dorset Primavera.*

OPPOSITE PAGE *The fairy-tale mural envelops the best seats in the dining room.*

BELOW, FROM TOP TO BOTTOM *The imperial staircase leading up to the restaurant; whitewashed exteriors betray the colonial décor inside.*

how its changing hues are reflected on the sand and crashing water below and allow yourself to be reassured that it was indeed a good idea to visit Puerto Rico.

ROOMS

The twenty-two Primavera suites are the older of the hotel's offering and remain its most charming. The 1,400-square-foot duplex suites feature deliciously comfortable king-size beds, private terraces with warm plunge pools, chaise longues, and small breakfast tables. Furnishings run the gamut of Caribbean colonial influences—Spanish, French, Dutch, and English—relying heavily on Caribbean mahogany and teak. The stone floors are painted a white-and-russet checkerboard pattern while woven floor rugs keep it cozy. Painted ceramic lamps with Venetian shades and tile-lined stairs up to the second floor bedroom are notable touches that point to diverse international influences, while ironwork sconces and chandeliers keep the Spanish theme the most prevalent. In December 2007, the hotel opened up seventeen newly redesigned beachfront residences that range in size from one to two bedrooms, though all with lavish marble bathrooms and a distinct Moroccan-style décor. The most secluded residence, appropriately named Casa Escondida (Hidden House), encompasses four suites around one central courtyard, complete with Moroccan lanterns and fountain. Despite the oversize showers and attractive mirrors in the new residence bathrooms, I'm still partial to the

Primavera suites, especially the cliffside ones (specifically number 45). Closest to the infinity pool on the left, number 45 shares only one wall with a neighbor, making its terrace area considerably more private. The room's four-poster bed with pillow-top mattress and its enormous soaking tub are two unforgettable elements—particularly for those on romantic holidays. The Poggesi shampoos and creams feature an appropriately yummy coconut-mango fragrance, while the marble bathroom furnishings cover the majority of the female-comfort requisites: double vanities, an extra table for an oversize toiletries bag, plus a shelf for quick-access items and a powerful magnifying mirror. Equipped with minifridges and Nespresso coffee makers, the rooms allow you the ability to shut yourself in, order room service at all hours, and completely ignore the outside world. There's even a charming tassel policy; hang the red one out on the doorknob for privacy, the green for cleaning. The resort is best enjoyed by amorous couples, given its minimal electronic amenities (no televisions or Internet access in the Primavera rooms) and subdued ambience. The service at the resort is another source of pride, and rightfully so. Everyone from the front desk to the waitstaff to the gardener is visibly willing to please. Unless surfing is a passion (Rincón is heralded for its high surf), two nights nestled inside the elegant Horned Dorset Primavera is all you need to relax, rejuvenate, or rekindle the flame.

CLOCKWISE FROM TOP LEFT *Spanish-style furnishings in dark stained wood create the Old World ambience; the inviting blue tile walls of the café restaurant; the ever-present palm trees in front of the guest rooms; the luxurious soaking tubs in the guest bathrooms.*

Deep feather beds, gauzy bed curtains, and doors open to the sea view ensure a good night's rest.

ISLE DE FRANCE

ST. BARTHS

Set on one of Saint Barthélemy's most attractive beaches, Baie des Flamands, the fashionable Hotel St.-Barth Isle de France welcomes its visitors with a tucked-away elegance and casual chic. The white, latticed portico entrance offset by enormous potted whitewashed bamboo, a French-blue railing, and a gleaming marble floor instantly alleviate any leftover jitters from your treacherous airplane landing and steep descent to the hotel. The informal front desk, an alcove off the front porch, keeps the mood light and airy during check-in while the sea air wafts down the hallway to massage away any impatience. Isle de France boasts one of the best entryway views of the sea. Framed perfectly by the white-on-white open-air hallway, charming Provençal-style blue pillows on the opposing couches, and swaying potted palms, that first glimpse of turquoise water and white powder beach beyond is oh-so-soothing. The simple, fresh décor of the main building is instantly inviting to newcomers and, no doubt, comforting for the regulars (no wonder Thanksgiving time is booked solid with repeat guests).

The relatively small dimensions of the main building, which include just twelve beach rooms and suites, create a homey element to the property, which is augmented by a shared bookcase of tattered paperbacks and my favorite amenity, a well-sourced boutique filled with coveted swimwear, sandals, and everything in between. Should anything have been left behind or you just can't resist the urge, the stylish boutique offers everything both men and women need to blend into tony St. Barths. Don't miss the weekly cocktail-hour fashion show where many of the top (read: skimpy) items are paraded around the restaurant and pool deck area by the boutique's owner and friends. Nothing quite says St. Barths like sipping a glass of pink champagne while beautiful bodies circulate.

The hotel's seaside French cuisine restaurant, La Case de l'Isle, and executive chef Bruce Domain do an excellent job with the transitions of the day. From a full European-style breakfast buffet with freshly baked mini-croissants and various fruits to beachside lunch service (the tuna tartare with French fries is well worth it) to candlelit dinner (make sure someone orders the chocolate soufflé), the restaurant remains an alluring spot to dine in, even if it is for the third time that day. (The cute waiters don't hurt, either.) The surrounding deck features white market umbrellas and banquette seating with block-printed blue-and-white pillows staying effortlessly stylish from daytime through evening. The righthand corner area hangs over the beach and with its driftwood bench and coffee table, it's the ideal spot for a cocktail any time of the day.

The small bar area or the boutique is where you'll likely run into the sun-kissed owners, Charles and Mandie Vere Nicoll, who bought the place in 2000 and have since made vast improvements, including a Molton Brown spa and four brand-new modern beach suites. Reverend Vere Nicoll is also the island's resident vicar and his charm and wit are just as much the bait that keeps the guests returning as the hotel itself.

ROOMS

Of the thirty-seven well-dressed rooms at the Isle de France, the ones that will capture your heart most effortlessly are the second-floor Beach Junior suites located in the main building. Overlooking the teak deck pool and the cerulean sea, the four upstairs beach suites offer an unobstructed view of paradise and, pleasantly, less overheard chatter than those suites below. Their wooden decks fit two generously sized chaise longues, a small couch, and a trolley bar stocked with ice-cold drinks and snacks. Outdoor breakfast tables for two beg for room service while the loungers get sun only in the afternoon, providing a pleasantly cool place to read in the morning. My favorite furnishing is in room 5. A small armless chair upholstered in a linen cloth with a red stripe down the center and the letters *M* and *E* on either side, it's the very epitome of shabby-chic. Room 9 is my top choice, with its large, inviting bed adorned with percale gray-and-red French fabric pillows and quilt and a delicate wooden writer's desk that awaits your postcard correspondence or littering of sunscreen bottles. The sky-blue wall color, polished white floors, and country-style furnishings (armoire with television inside) mix the minimal demands of Caribbean design with the sophisticated look of southern France. The spacious bathroom is done in traditional marble

PREVIOUS PAGE   *Colorful Indian-print cushions spruce up the casual, outdoor dining at Isle de France.*

ABOVE   *The resort's well-shaded hamlet on secluded Flamands Bay in Saint Barths.*

OPPOSITE PAGE   *The hotel's teak-decked pool is no stranger to bathing beauties.*

with a bathtub and separate rain shower; though sadly the bathroom has no window, there is a skylight. Above all, the room is clean and pretty, and if you're happiest in very feminine rooms, then this, too, will be your top choice.

The rest of the hotel's twenty-four rooms are located across from the main building and nestled back into the hill and garden. Lusciously landscaped with an elevated teak promenade that winds through palms and bougainvillea, the property's backyard, so to speak, is a surprisingly wonderful alternative. With three garden rooms, twelve bungalows, and two suites, plus a secluded hillside cottage with pool that requires climbing

sixty-two steps, the garden rooms are the perfect choice for a small family or someone wanting total privacy. The Tropical Villa (room 23) features its own pool, separate sitting room, and an outdoor kitchenette with decorative glassware and savory Dean & DeLuca snacks. The fridge is well stocked with beverages (including champagne, juice, and diet soda) while the bathroom is a regular treasure trove of Molton Brown products. The showers are a bit tight and the toilet is sequestered European-style into its own closet in the hallway, but the towels, oh the towels . . . Their warmth, size, and fluffy goodness are divine. Equally memorable are the fine, crisp bed sheets with a

subtly embroidered duvet and plentiful goose-down pillows. Don't forget to turn off the pesky French-regulation pool alarm (unless, of course, there are children in your party)—its screeching siren can unsettle well-earned relaxation. Amusingly, its occurrence incites the birds into a cheerful response. Each room was decorated individually by interior designer Penny Morrison, whose heavy use of vintage French fabrics and smart choice of sheer linens in pale neutral tones create a pleasant harmony with the casual Caribbean French (read: non-scene-y) side of St. Barths.

Quilted French linens give a Provençal feel.

CLOCKWISE FROM LEFT   *A picture-perfect view from the main building's second-floor guest rooms; whitewashed wicker and mono-grammed towels in the bathrooms; another guest room done in pastel Provençal fashion; the beachside café.*

LE SERENO

ST. BARTHS

A chauffeured arrival, compliments of the hotel, ensures the proper approach to checking into St. Barths' latest "It Girl" property: Le Sereno. Fronting the breezy Anse de Grand Cul-de-Sac beach, neighboring the celebrated Guanahani Hotel and Spa, this glamorous property has all the requisite credentials for its fast track to fame. Whether it's the stunning Hugh Newell Jacobsen–like reception house, with its bright red doors and arresting view of reclining palms and aqua-blue waters, or the guest rooms' recent facelift from acclaimed French interior designer Christian Liaigre, Le Sereno is guaranteed to make you a bit goo-goo-eyed upon first impression. Descending the whitewashed deck staircase from the check-in area down to the teak deck pool merits a soundtrack—Edith Piaf, Django Reinhardt, or, if it's an evening arrival, then perhaps a sample off a St. Germain mix would work, but all definitively French. Once on ground level, follow the deck path, passing by the linen-filled Blanc Bleu boutique on the right and the louvered windows of the bar on the left, directly out to the soft, white, sandy beach. The consistent breeze on the Grand Cul-de-Sac bay caters perfectly to the water-sport enthusiast and thus, kite surfers and wind surfers can be seen whipping by all day long, adding even more cachet to an already mesmerizing scene.

The stream-lined, fresh-water pool is the visual focal point and nerve center of the hotel. With beige-striped cushioned pool loungers lining both sides, lanky palm trees sprouting from the teak deck, and surrounding grass landscape, the pool's sleek design is impressive, though best appreciated uninhabited. Be sure to drop your towel off early in the morning to claim one of chaises on the opposite side of the restaurant and closest to the beach—they get the best sun throughout the day. Although the hotel is actually located left of center on the horseshoe-shaped bay, the hotel's uneven layout—more guest rooms are to the left of the restaurant—and the pool appear to offer a centered view of the glittering bay. At night, the property truly shines with alternating LED color lighting in the pool and orange and green floodlights at the base of a few palm trees. The restaurant and bar slip into their hip lounge role, though the area remains relaxed and is never the least bit obnoxious. The bartenders are fittingly St. Barths-attractive and serve their nurtured cocktails with a flourish and confident attitude that guarantees even the faint of heart will order a second. The bar area is located in the corner of the restaurant. Stark with simple wood furnishings and dark in both wood stain color and lighting—hurricane candles on the tables provide the only light—an evening cocktail is best enjoyed on the few daybeds on the pool deck. The open-air restaurant, Le Restaurant des Pêcheurs, faces the beach (with a few tables actually in the sand) and features a long, curved white banquette that shares a row of white table-tops with canvas deck chairs. Varnished hardwood floors and two moon-shaped wooden tables complete the yacht-like décor while the retractable shades guarantee that the enjoyment of the sea breezes are just as intimate. The cuisine is focused on serving the freshest fish in St. Barths, relying on the daily catch from the local fishermen and preparing it as simply as possible. The waiters delight in recommending dishes and their pride is clear from their detailed dish descriptions and thoughtful wine-pairing suggestions. Fortunately the restaurant, and most of St. Barths, imports much of its wine directly from France and thus options for wine are far better than most Caribbean islands. Be sure to take advantage here, where the wine prices are not as typically inflated for St. Barths. The restaurant is home to the entire day's roster of meals; the changeover between daytime and nighttime is seamless and what was earlier a casual, sometimes sand-strewn floor becomes an elegant, heels-appropriate setting at night.

ROOMS

The guest rooms at Le Sereno can be most easily distinguished by their fresh and straightforward décor. Simple, stark furnishings presented in the same monochromatic palette as the dining room, with dark wood floors, and whitewashed walls, allow the rooms to serve as backdrops for the bright colors of the outdoors. Surrounded by pink and orange bougainvillea and feathering traveler's palms, the thirty-seven suites fan the property's seafront and range from garden rooms to deluxe suites, including two beachfront cottages with soaking

tubs, large porches, and direct beach access. Two styles of architecture divide the room categories, making a more tailored experience possible. The garden rooms, set just behind the pool, are whitewashed adobe-style buildings with front porches, evoking a hint of Santorini and ideal for the convivial traveler. The ocean-front rooms located to the left of the restaurant are set up much like a row of beach cabanas, with canvas dividers and park benches just outside the doors. I'm partial to the second set, and with their sweeping views, increased privacy, and subdued sophistication, it's hard not to be.

The room décor is sort of a cosmopolitan-beach hybrid, or "beach cabana meets refined contemporary." The layout is open so that upon entering the eye travels quickly beyond the custom four-poster bed, over the modern settee-couch, and right through the sliding glass doors to an aqua-blue water view. (Although the cabana rooms sit on the water's edge, they have no direct access to the beach.) Pinpoints of Liaigre's sleek, modern style can be seen in the clean lines of the furniture; the wardrobe's simple white-on-dark wood; the flared-leg writing desk with branch-inspired chair, which is easily the most decorative element in the room; and the brown nylon luggage bench at the foot of the bed. In keeping with the requisites for a luxury hotel, the rooms are predictably equipped with flat-screen televisions and iPod docking stations. The feeling of elegance can be found within the four-poster beds, whose crisp linens were designed exclusively by Porthault, and mosquito-net canopies create that magical, only-in-the-tropics feel. The perfectly fluffed pillows remind you that you are somewhere where the staff is attentive while the minimally adorned walls encourage you to unpack right away in order to add accents. Given the lack of decorative elements (a sole hurricane lamp on the coffee table and an orchid plant on the desk), adding your piles of brightly colored clothes, books, and toiletries recalls decorating blank dorm rooms—but way, *way* better. Despite the cabana-thin walls, getting to sleep is relatively easy, and when the bright morning sunlight illuminates the room, it instantly reminds you of your privileged location. The bathrooms are tucked behind the bedroom—never my favorite hotel layout since it often means an absence of natural light. But these bathrooms are a delight, with their louvered windows, teak shower floors, multiple wall hooks (ideal for wet bathing suits), and enough counter space for all the extra creams Caribbean vacations entail. Room 25 falls somewhere in the middle of the row, offering a central view across the bay and a copper outdoor shower with pull-chain lever for quick rinses. If you're so inclined, the hip-level shrubbery could allow for the immodest to shower in the buff, though it doesn't shield from your direct neighbors—but then again, you're practically in France anyway. Given the relative simplicity of the rooms, the onus is on the guest to add the color. In turn, the room keeps its promise as an attractive stage set patiently awaiting your arrival.

Author's addendum: The hotel has recently added three new four-bedroom villas also designed by Christian Liaigre. The bi-level villas are over 7,000-square-feet each and feature private pools, gourmet kitchens, and expansive patios, not to mention twenty-four-hour butler service.

PREVIOUS PAGE   *Even when windswept, the pool area at Le Sereno cries chic.*

OPPOSITE PAGE, FROM LEFT TO RIGHT   *A wood-trimmed bathtub in a suite; simple, fresh bed linens.*

ABOVE   *Exhibitionists will delight in the rinse shower of the waterfront guest rooms.*

OPPOSITE PAGE   *Breezy nights at Le Sereno only add to the enchantment.*

ABOVE, LEFT TO RIGHT   *Lipstick-red doors announce a guest's entry; Christian Liaigre's minimal décor in the guest room.*

MAISON NOUREEV

ST. BARTHS

An island hideaway unlike any other, Maison Noureev is a testament to the idea of an island house intended primarily for personal sanctuary. Truly and utterly isolated on the rocky, southeastern shoreline of St. Barths, the mid-century wooden cottage stands alone on its stretch of seaside road, resolute, with its shredded yellow banner flag flapping in the unrelenting breeze. The house earns its moniker from its previous owner, the renowned ballet dancer Rudolf Nureyev, who customized an enormous deck (approximately forty feet long and ten feet wide) so he could dance facing out to the sea. Located in an undeveloped area known as Grand Fond and buffered on one side by national parkland and on the other by coastline that would be impossible to build on, the house is totally protected from the threat of neighbors, just as its former owner preferred, and a feeling shared by its current owner, the kind and generous Jeanne Audy-Rowland.

The seaside home is a marvel in utilitarian design, allowing up to eight guests to gather comfortably and reside peacefully, and even separately, despite its relatively tight square footage. Divided into a series of three dwellings—the main house, the Datcha, and the guest cottage—the house provides various refuges and tiny enclaves ideal for indulging in some quiet time, that is, if you can ever tear yourself away from the expansive deck and its mesmerizing 180-degree sea view or come out of the salt-water pool fed directly from the sea. Designed as an extension of the house, the deck, with its multiple levels, secluded corners, and inviting teak furniture, is the true heart of the house, which is only fitting, given its illustrious beginnings. The weather-beaten exterior of the house has been delightfully decorated with the current owner's charming yellow script detailing everything from the names of each room to cautionary instructions on steps to lines of poetry—all in French of course. A mixture of stone and stripped wood, the low-slung house befits its environment, bearing neither a trace of garishness nor hint of ostentation. Rather, both the exterior and interior pay heed to their vulnerable seafront position by allowing the wood to weather and the furnishings to remain simple. Reminiscent of a nineteenth-century whaling house, the library-living room is a hodgepodge of antique furnishings, brass chandeliers, cracked leather sofas covered with white sheets thrown over them for protection (and possibly comfort), various objets d'art, and even a hammock and Nureyev's upright piano in the corner. The house remains almost as Nureyev left it. "It's his house, not mine," Jeanne is oft heard repeating. The effect is simple and worn—perfect for relaxing alongside the sea.

The kitchen, another core area of the main house, is totally French influenced. Porcelain teacups of varying sizes hang from a glassless wall cabinet while large spice jars, clay and tin mugs, and plates and bowls of different colors evoke Provence from the open shelves over the kitchen counter. The hanging shelf over the sink, topped with more plates and dangling crystal glasses, solidifies the country-style motif. If the weather behaves, both breakfast and lunch are eaten outside on the deck's warped wooden table overlooking the sea. Lunchtime can get a bit hot, so save yourself a seat under the umbrella. Dinner is best appreciated around the large, round dining table in the kitchen, which dresses up nicely with the owner's collection of fine, antique lace cloths. And with candles flickering and the wind howling at the door, the mood is unmistakably, nineteenth-century European.

The idea behind staying at Maison Noureev is to unwind and spend quality time with chosen company, away from the hubbub that befalls St. Barths. That said, it's also wonderfully situated near Saline Beach, which offers one of the most spectacular white-sand enclaves in the Caribbean, plus some good dining options should a meal out feel necessary. Heading in the direction of Saint Jean, there's a darling patisserie called Saint Hélène Boulangerie, which sells oven-warm croissants and baguettes to ensure the day's meals begin on a fresh note. They deliver to some of the closer bakeries but you must get to the patisserie early, or as the locals say, before the tourists wake up.

ROOMS

With a total of five rooms, the house is best suited for six or eight, provided the last two don't mind staying down below or in the tiny captain's room. Decorated simply and swathed in white linen and Egyptian cotton—a signature textile of the current owner—the rooms are as romantic as the setting itself. Assisted by mosquito netting, sleeping is done with the doors wide open to the breeze and bright moonlight. The master bedroom, or Chambre de Jeanne, as it's affectionately called, occupies the enviable corner wing and is a bit more sheltered from the unrelenting breeze. However, the Chambre de Nicolas is my favorite. With its generously sized bed, antique linen shams, and heavily cushioned teak steamer chair looking right out to the sea, the room is a haven in its own right. Its bathroom is also the house's best, with a standing rain shower and well-lit sink area. In her former life, the sparkling owner made beautiful scented soaps—whose recipe has since been sold to the local spa line, Ligne St. Barth—but luckily there were some saved that are available for her fortunate guests. The Datcha, which means "Russian country house," looks anything but and is instead a smaller cabin to the left of the main house with its own bathroom, outside shower, and small kitchenette. The bedroom is not quite as exposed or finely decorated as the Chambre de Nicolas, but the added privacy and private deck with chaise longues and small garden make it an amorous couple's top choice. The downstairs bedroom is also a preferred lair for some, offering complete privacy from the guests above, while the small captain's room is best left for decoration or the last-minute overnight guest. The rooms are not luxurious in terms of modern amenities but rather in their natural setting, proximity to the sea, and comfort of the world before flat-screen televisions became requisite. Blissfully removed from the maddening world (though an Internet connection is surprisingly available and there are two in-house televisions), the house seems to answer the call of the overburdened. For a spot to truly unplug, sleep soundly, and simply relax, there's no more natural a spot.

Given the unfettered appeal of the house, it's no surprise it has been the backdrop in countless fashion spreads from *Elle* to Hermès. The setting is truly distinct and the aura of romance palpable. To rush or worry as a guest at Maison Noureev would be incongruous to the framework and soul of the house; it would be like stomping on Nureyev's grave. As Nureyev grew increasingly private as time passed, it's purported that he never performed publicly in St. Barths; instead, he preferred to invite the local children over to his house, have them sit in the deck's inlaid bleacher steps, and watch as he floated and jumped across his teak stage. A haven for the dancer, particularly in his final year when he spent five weeks here just before the doctors called him back to Paris, where he eventually died, the place remains a refuge—soothing and restoring to all its visitors.

la chambre du voyageur

CLOCKWISE FROM TOP LEFT   *A heavily cushioned chaise in the guest room; one of Jeanne's many hand-painted signs; the entrance to the master suite; the French-country kitchen complete with labeled jars and dangling mugs.*

ABOVE   *The infamous porch where Noureev performed for the locals.*

FOLLOWING PAGES   *Maison Noureev—in constant communication with the sea.*

VILLA LA DANSE DES ETOILES

ST. BARTHS

The owners of Villa la Danse des Etoiles (Dance of the Stars) said it best when they described their newest villa on St. Barths as an "architectural statement." With perhaps the most stunning location on the island, atop of the northernmost point, the villa makes a statement, particularly to its neighbors. While driving around the sharp bends and random inclines of Pointe Milou, the blur of one white house after another can get disorienting. Luckily for drivers across St. Barths, Villa le Danse des Etoiles broke the mold and in turn has become both a testament to modern architecture and a useful landmark. Built with imported Pennsylvanian fieldstone (the same stone used in the owners' Long Island, New York, home) and combined with a zinc roof, cement columns, and ipe decking, the exterior of the house is a true departure from the norm. Traditionally the roofs of St. Barths are red or green, and this villa's roof is unlike any other on the island, while the black volcanic lava stone from Indonesia lining both the pool and its overflow area introduces another tropical tone to the French Caribbean style of St. Barths.

Walking up the villa's stairs to the side door, especially after your car has barely stayed in gear around the hairpin turn into the driveway, feels a bit off balance. Where is the grand entrance to such an architectural feat? Instead, there's a sliding glass door with a teak frame that opens into the kitchen. Upon entering, though, the plainness of the entrance is quickly replaced with awe for the utter immensity of the view. A heavy reliance on glass windows and sliding doors (the glass came from Maine) allows for the panorama to follow you from one end of the house to the other. From the villa's prominent hilltop location, guests are treated to front-row views of both sunset and sunrise while the house and its core materials absorb the constant changes in the light.

The kitchen is a stark, modern affair with polished gray countertops and a separate island made from a mix of cement and French white gravel. Slight variations of the contemporary LEM piston bar stool in gray leather line two sides of the island, while a mahogany dining room table for ten with black leather chairs lies just beyond. The refrigerator is hidden within the wall of floor-to-ceiling cabinets made locally of Brazilian hardwood sucupira. The floors are done in coumaron, while the windows are framed in teak and mahogany. With three various types of wood at play in the central room, it is clear that each selection was thoughtfully and purposely made. Paired with the wood are stone walls laid in an uneven line with extra-wide grout so that some appear to be sticking out of the wall —a specific method requested by the owner and learned by the local workforce. According to the villa's builder, Xavier David, masons worked full time for over two years on the house's unique construction. The kitchen, dining room, and living room are grouped together into one large space with fifteen-foot ceilings, which also fit a narrow loft space customized into an office with a built-in desk. This space is surprisingly comfortable and the open view overlooking the living room and out the ten-foot sliding glass doors keeps the hard worker's island view always in sight. The staircase up to the loft is emblematic of the sleek, modern style of the house's décor. The combination of a stainless-steel banister and sucupira floating stairs against the uneven stone-wall backdrop carries the "architectural feat" theme indoors. Furnishings in the family room-living room lean toward the simple, with two white slip-covered couches, a large, square coffee table, and two equally plush white chairs. The main accent of the room is Kartell Bourgie lamps on the two side tables. Their transparent polycarbonate material plays perfectly with the light streaming into the space, and their modern design maintains the uncluttered and airy feel of the room. Encased in the other floor-to-ceiling sucupira cabinet is the flat-screen television, ensuring that modernity and creature comforts are fundamental to the home's design. The best part of the room, though, is its retractable sliding glass back wall. With some help—it's a bit heavy and watch your fingers—the entire back wall will fold up to one side like an accordian, allowing for total interaction between the outdoors and the indoors.

A very important element of this "architectural feat" is its attention to green-friendly energy sources. There are solar panels on top of the roof that are used to heat the villa's water supply and special pipes to redirect and control the runoff from the air-conditioner. According to the builder, Villa la Danse des Etoiles uses fifty percent less energy than houses built on the island in the 1990s.

Given the relatively small indoor living space, the attention paid to the outdoor living area is understood. A combination of ipe wood decking and laid-slate flooring maintains the cool, almost industrial tone. On one side of the deck is an almost entire replica of the indoor gathering area: a six-person dining table and seated cocktail area with teak lounge chairs stuffed with white cushions, all kept safely in the shade under the zinc roof. The six-range outdoor grill completes the functional design. On the other side, divided by freestanding stone walls, is the master bedroom's secluded deck area with two teak chaises. Beyond the private nook is an enclosed grassy space with an outdoor billiards table and a powder room with shower. While the placement feels a bit odd, given that the master bedroom's area is smack in between where people gather and the pool table, the circular maze design of the bathroom and its platinum mirror, not to mention the very gumption of having a pool table exposed to the elements, keeps the mood haphazardly childlike and fun.

Glistening beyond the impressive furniture layout is the villa's true pièce de résistance: the seventy-foot-long, crescent-shaped infinity pool and its postcard-perfect view. Cushioned loungers frame the front of the westward-facing pool while a mesh-fabric set basks beneath its runoff, offering a more private option for sunbathing. It was with every ounce of discipline that I forced myself to leave those poolside chaises and their spellbinding picture-perfect view. Again, to quote the owner, "The design evolved as a means of framing the view…and when you are in the house, you feel like you are the only one in the world!" I happily second his comments and add that not only do you feel like you are solitary, there's an unmistakable (and irresistible) sense of power derived from commanding that view, too.

ROOMS

The surprisingly compact villa has just three bedrooms, all with king-size beds that can be converted to twins. Each room feels separate from the other through varying layouts and exterior private gardens. In pondering a fourth bedroom, the owner opted instead to focus on designing distinct common areas. The rooms are all equally attractive with flat-screen televisions, iPod docks, air-conditioning, ceiling fans, and leather-upholstered bed frames, and though the signature view is certainly given to the master bedroom, my favorite is the room at the very front of the house. With its woven coconut-shell bed frame, mahogany floor-to-ceiling closet doors, and clean whitewashed walls, this bedroom seems warm and natural whereas the stone walls of the master bedroom can feel a bit too cold for my taste. The middle room, with its mirrored back wall, is a pleasant room but a bit tighter in dimensions and with a smaller bathroom. Although every room's bathroom features tiled floors, the same gravel-and-cement counter-

tops, and Kohler fixtures, the front bedroom's outside shower setup and generous counter space is instantly more inviting. With an unobstructed eastern view out to the ocean and a small rock island in the distance, the romance magnifies with every day's washing. (Note that the only shower in the room is the outdoor one and it's best to choose your shower time when the driveway traffic is at a standstill.) Overall, the bedroom aesthetic is structured and cool, much like the villa's main room. The same stone and hardwood continues throughout and can feel a bit impersonal without the addition of one's personal effects. It is clear that this house was built with the purpose of renting, since it follows the standard rules of equally sized rooms and modern amenities (there's also Wi-Fi throughout the house). There's also a distinctly masculine feel to the décor with a heavy influence of core building materials and sparse decorative elements. The potted orchids seem to be the only feminine touch and, given their popularity in corporate hotels, the ambience still feels a bit stiff. However, if all of this is making you second-guess your selection of this very cool, ultra-sleek villa, take a deep breath, unpack your colorful clothing, and then retire immediately to any one of the umpteen loungers. I promise, after ten minutes of soaking in the view, any hesitancy towards such bold, contemporary design will melt away and you'll find yourself basking in the glory of modern improvements.

CLOCKWISE FROM TOP LEFT *A stone goat marks one of the few artistic embellishments; the varying textures continue in the guest rooms; the contemporary style of the living room; sliding wood doors reveal the bathroom suite.*

The master bedroom's terrace loungers.

JADE MOUNTAIN

ST. LUCIA

*U*nlike any other property in the world, Jade Mountain is both a futuristic marvel and flourishing complement to St. Lucia's vibrant landscape. The striking (and somewhat curious) design is the completed vision of architect (and owner) Nick Troubetzkoy, who came to St. Lucia in the 1970s and has been held captive by the Pitons ever since. Named after Nick's personal collection of antique carved jade mountains, the astounding, 35,000-plus-square-foot property is, as his wife puts it, Nick's own carved Jade Mountain, where he hopes to not only showcase the dramatic scenery of the Pitons, St. Lucia's majestic twin peaks, but also give the onlooker the sensation that he or she is floating alongside them. As a result, the conceptualized architecture is inherently unique: towering stone columns, known as Columns to Heaven, soar up into the air and support narrow bridges, known as Bridges to Infinity, which link to the multi-leveled main structure, whose rounded edges and open walls jut out toward the Pitons. Escher-esque with crisscrossing bridges, multiple staircases, and louvered windows, the building, if you can call it that, is genuinely awe-inspiring. Built into the side of a lush hill, the property's massive, rough concrete exterior and cut-stone walls strike a sharp contrast with the verdant jungle and surrounding bougainvillea. In an effort to reintroduce color and use recycled materials, Nick enlisted the help of David Knox of Lightstreams to create colored glass designs that affix to the top of each column, along with handmade, iridescent pool tiles (whose mold was destroyed, ensuring their one-of-a-kind status) that line the reflecting pools that wiggle around the property. The hotel has hardly remained under the radar, due to its captivatingly complicated design and award-winning use of local construction and recycled materials; however, the rooms, known as sanctuaries, are veritable hideaways themselves.

Once you've adjusted your eyes to the *Jetsons*-esque structure, the immediate impulse is to explore. Fortunately, your personal *majordomo* appears at check-in and escorts you to your room, explaining how no request is too big or too small, from unpacking and later packing your clothes to arranging a candlelit dinner on your balcony to booking the in-house photographer. He'll also explain the color-coded bandanna sign system that hangs from the door and signals the staff to either fulfill a request or not disturb and then leaves you with a tiny cell phone that will reach him at any hour. Once you see the rooms, with their fifteen-foot-high ceilings and truly otherworldly view, it's hardly surprising to note that most doors carry the customary "go away" red bandannas on their hooks throughout the day. Just down the hill is the property's sister resort, Anse Chastanet, where Jade Mountain guests enjoy the full privileges of its three restaurants, black sandy beach, and various water sports including world-class dive sites. The newest activity, jungle biking with Tyson, can be as challenging as you desire, and is informative as well, given that you bike through ruins of the old rum plantation. Even more exercise, should you want it, is available through daily yoga classes taught on the sky-scraping roof deck, where sun salutations take on a whole new relevancy, and in a new, air-conditioned gym with all the latest equipment. For those who've come to worship the sun on their bodies, there's also a quiet beach, located on the next bay (with the same entry point for jungle biking), which is ideal for couples seeking that marooned feeling. As the property's literature does warn, there are approximately one-hundred steps up from Anse Chastanet to Jade Mountain (sometimes more if your sanctuary is on the top level); luckily, your majordomo is on call and will gladly bring any item you may have forgotten down to the beach. The terrace restaurant at Jade Mountain is exclusive to Jade Mountain guests, occupying the top floor of the property and featuring a circular central pool and separate lounge area used during cocktails and afternoon tea (freshly baked cookies!). The food and ambience are better at night than midday (when most guests are usually indulging in the privacy of room service or down at the beach anyway), and the evening becomes magical when the saxophonist plays and the fiery sunset light reflects off the multicolored, iridescent tiles in the pool.

187

PREVIOUS PAGE   *The magnificent peaks, the Pitons, on view from every angle in guest room JE1.*

BELOW, FROM TOP TO BOTTOM   *The iridescent, one-of-a-kind pool tiles; a batik bedspread.*

OPPOSITE PAGE   *Manmade and natural wonders side by side.*

ROOMS

Divided into three categories appropriately named Star, Moon, and Sun, the sanctuary suites get bigger as you climb closer to the sun, though all feature infinity pools and superlative views of the Pitons and the sea. Jade Mountain sanctuaries glean their otherworldliness from the lack of two exterior walls. The rooms are left completely open to the elements on one side, allowing high soaring birds to make frequent appearances inside the rooms—the bold ones will even bathe in the top steps of the room's infinity pool. (Beware of leaving food out, as they can be scavengers). Fortunately, the rooms' glamorous proportions of fourteen-foot-ceilings, a multitude of ceiling fans (eleven in my room!), and cliffside location keep bugs notably away. Nick's intent was to create not only signature rooms that transport their guests into the view but also suites that are as harmonious with the surroundings as possible. Locally made wood furnishings mix with popular island-style pieces from Janus et Cie and Padma's Plantation. The walls and floors feature crushed blush-toned coral plaster and quarried coral tile from neighboring islands. The louvered windows and mullions are finished with over twenty different tropical hardwoods carefully harvested from the rain forest in Guyana. Sanctuary JE1, a Sun-level suite, is easily the best suite in the house, though it appears every guest feels that way about his or her own room. The 2,000-square-foot room features 270-degree views and a massive, 900-square-foot infinity pool dangling off the western-facing edge, aimed right at the sunset. Watching the sun dip into the sea from the pool's curved edge offers the exact sensation that Nick was after—a feeling of rare intimacy with nature's magnificence. Immediately upon entry, the grand size of the room and its absence of walls (this suite is technically missing two) really does make you feel as if you're floating into the jaw-dropping view. The open layout allows sitting areas to flow into one another while the tile-lined, gurgling pool appears to ebb directly from the room's hardwood floor and fall off into the sea. The king-size four-poster bed is swathed in butterfly netting with Frette sheets and whimsically decorated with batik throw pillows and coverlet. The morning light serves as the alarm clock given the lack of shades (or walls) and even if the bed weren't as heavenly soft as it is, it would be a struggle to rise from the unadulterated view of the Pitons seen right from your pillow. The elevated bathroom buffered by a commanding, Jacuzzi bathtub with its own LED lighting sits tucked out of view with a tile shower and porcelain Duravit sinks. Purposely techno-free, the suites cater to those looking to unplug completely and invest in quality time with nature, themselves, and whomever they may have brought. I easily imagined spending an entire week in just the room, blissfully content to have nothing but the captivating view and my husband for entertainment. The epic scenery and fascinating layout of Jade Mountain allow guests to be entirely absorbed by their surroundings, and fabulously transported from whatever you came to Jade Mountain to escape.

OPPOSITE PAGE *Jade Mountain's beguiling and marvelous architecture.*

ABOVE *Infinity pools in the guest rooms give the feeling of floating directly into the horizon.*

LADERA

ST. LUCIA

*F*ew places in the Caribbean islands can declare, without hesitation, that they have the most dramatic, stop-in-your-tracks type of view—St. Lucia's Ladera can. Built high into the top of a lush mountain ridge and facing out over Piton Bay, the twenty-seven-suite property scored center-row seats for the most stunning (and adored) act in town, the two volcanic points known as the

Pitons. Part of a World Heritage site, the Pitons, volcanic plugs formed when magma hardened within a vent on an active volcano, rise up from the ocean in sheer granite defiance, taunting and amazing all who come to gawk. The Petit Piton is actually taller than Gros Piton, though both beckon climbers with their foreboding shape and curious vegetation (some sides are pure rock while others are quite verdant). For the non-climbers, their beauty is stunning to observe, particularly in the early morning and, naturally, at sunset.

Set up in on one long plane across the ridge, Ladera's lodgelike structure is marked by endless woodcarvings, cut stone, intricate mosaic tile work, and, of course, open views out to the beach of Anse de Pitons and the sparkling emerald bay. Built by American architect John DiPol, who is credited with bringing the first power tools to the island, the three-acre French plantation–style resort has arguably the best location in the Caribbean. The famous "missing fourth wall" design is a signature aspect of Ladera's natural style and promotes their intent of living as a guest of Mother Nature. As a result, there is little to no divide between guests and all of Mother Nature's children. In fact, in the terrace dining room, plastic water guns are left

on the tables to shoo the pesky birds from your food. (Luckily, water guns are still funno matter your age.) Fortunately, the birds are long gone by cocktail hour when a light breeze swirls through the hills, ensuring an evening meal of unencumbered romance. The central two-story main building features the award-winning Dasheene restaurant, where the charming chef Orlando, a James Beard-honoree, loves to impress. Ask him to prepare his signatures: the trio of soup (calaloo, pumpkin and coconut broths) and the coconut crème brûlée, and his ego won't allow him to disappoint. Beneath the restaurant and in front of the darling hotel shop (where local art and cedar woodcarvings are in abundance) is the convivial, circular green-heart-wood-slatted bar and ample lounge area with a bright, mosaic tile floor done by St. Lucian artisans. Dark wicker chair sets with carved woodblock tables are staggered apart and angled to drink in the view. On some nights the hotel hosts a four-piece reggae band on the lounge terrace, enabling unabashed guests to dance and even sing along. The hotel's eco-conscious mindset attracts the type of laid-back guests who commonly wield backpacks, while its breathtaking vista, sulfur spring spa, and lauded dining appease those intent upon peace

and romance. Hand-carved wooden signs characterize the property (and direct guests) along with brightly colored mosiacs featuring elaborate marine designs. The ambience is quite serene, given most guests are couples (the missing wall makes this spot not ideal for young children) who either spend long hours in their suites, out on hikes, or down at the beach (whose white sand was imported from the north of the island), where there are complimentary chairs and a full-service restaurant. Capitalizing on its romantic setting, the resort has a new, 1,200-square-foot Paradise Pavilion to host weddings of up to one hundred people. Fortunately for those who have traveled to Ladera seeking peace and quiet, this pavilion is tucked off to the side of the resort and connected to one of the Hilltop Dream suites (X8) by a private pathway. It's easy to enter into a bit of a lulled stupor or forget the day of the week at Ladera—its optimal setting at 1,100 feet in the air and intimate, lodgelike design make it impossible for guests to resist the Pitons' magical spell.

ROOMS

All twenty-seven suites and villas at Ladera lack a fourth wall, guaranteeing unobstructed views of the Pitons, not to mention a constant communication with nature. (Beware—if you're not comfortable with bugs that buzz or frogs and lizards, this is not the spot for you.) Constructed in cut stone and tropical hardwoods, mainly greenheart from the neighboring rain forest, the rooms look and feel like Polynesian tree houses.

PREVIOUS PAGE   *Quirky, wood-carved details like double swings abound in the guestrooms at Ladera.*

ABOVE   *Breakfast at Ladera offers direct communication with nature.*

OPPOSITE PAGE   *The Petit Piton on view from the pool.*

Louvered doors, wood floors, and gabled ceilings lend them a typical Caribbean flavor but the abundance of intricate woodcarvings and pottery reliefs on every surface, from each suite's sink basin to the columns to even the dish rack, give the rooms their own, distinct character. Each of the suites has a dip pool—some larger than others—with wooden chair swings for a whimsical seat with a view and four-poster beds draped in netting, which is an absolute necessity here. The remaining furniture is a mixture of nineteenth-century French and cushioned wicker seating. Villa G, a three-bedroom villa, has a spacious duplex layout. The master bedroom faces out to the open view, as does its shower, sink, and toilet.

Unfortunately this means that once the sun has set, any light you leave on (like the one over the sink) becomes quickly infested with moths. If you're crafty, though, you can use it as a bug magnet and sleep soundly knowing they're attracted elsewhere. The downstairs area fits a sitting area, a six-person dining table, a wet bar, and a generous porch with lounge chairs. The pool, however, is back by the entrance, flowing like a lagoon from the front door to under the staircase to behind the sofa. It is a great place for families with older kids, given all the space, while the multiple bathrooms (I used the hallway bathroom rather than the master to store my toiletries and brush my teeth at night) keep

everyone comfortable. For couples, my pick would be Hilltop Dream Suite XVI for its split-level design, simply shaped pool, and spacious bathroom with walk-in mosaic tile shower. The sunken sitting room features a cushioned sofa and plantation chairs, ideal for when the swing grows tiresome or, to toast the evening sunset in privacy before dinner. The elevated, four-poster bed faces the view so that the first thing you see in the morning is the glorious, indelible sight of the steel-gray Pitons and the glistening green bay below. Try not to be bothered by the constant visiting birds; you'll hardly notice them by day two and by day three, you'll begin to feel like Cinderella surrounded by her friends.

The "missing fourth wall" in a duplex guestroom.

CLOCKWISE FROM TOP LEFT *The ornately carved bar; charming signs point guests to their destinations; tile work and clay sink basins in the bathrooms; polished floors, stone walls, and intricately crafted furnishings give Ladera's guest rooms a handcrafted and upscale tree-house feel.*

HIDEAWAYS INDEX

ANGUILLA

BIRD OF PARADISE VILLA
Anguilla, West Indies
Tel: 414-791-9461
www.anguillabird.com
Premiere
Beach, Pool, Private Chef,
Cooking Lessons

ANTIGUA

HERMITAGE BAY
St. Mary's, Antigua, West Indies
Tel: +1 (268) 562-5500
www.hermitagebay.com
Luxury
Beach, Pool, Watersports, Spa,
Inclusive plan

BARBADOS

COBBLERS COVE
Speightstown, St. Peter, Barbados
Tel: 246-422-2291
www.cobblerscove.com
Premiere
Beach, Pool, Inclusive Plan, Fine Dining,
Spa, Gym

FUSTIC HOUSE
St. Lucy, Barbados
Tel: +44 7802 254 718
www.fustichouse.com
Premiere
Private chef, Pool, Gardens, Marina and
Beach Club Access

BEQUIA

FIREFLY PLANTATION
Spring Bay, St. Vincent and the
Grenadines, West Indies
Tel: +1 (784) 458-3414
www.fireflybequia.com
Moderate
Pool, Working Plantation, Historic

BRITISH VIRGIN ISLANDS

FRENCHMAN'S LOOKOUT
Tortola, British Virgin Islands
Tel: (866) 940-0020
www.frenchmanslookout.com
Premiere
Pool, Private Chef, Watersports, Gym

STEELE POINT
Tortola, British Virgin Islands
Tel: +1 (610) 453-4488
www.steelepoint.com
Luxury
Pool, Watersports

AQUAMARE
Mahoe Bay, Virgin Gorda,
British Virgin Islands
Tel: +1 (787) 461-2638
www.villaaquamare.com
Premiere
Pool, Private Beach, Watersports

DOMINICAN REPUBLIC

PENINSULA HOUSE
Las Terrenas, Dominican Republic
Tel: +1 (809) 962-7447; +1 (809) 817-1152
www.thepeninsulahouse.com
Premiere
Pool, Beach Club, Fine Dining

GRENADA

BEL AIR PLANTATION
St. David's Point, Grenada
Tel: +1 (473) 444-6305; (866) 504-3359
www.belairplantation.com
Moderate
Pool, Watersports

LA LUNA
St. Georges, Grenada
Tel: +1 (473) 439-0001; (866) 452-5862
www.laluna.com
Luxury
Beach, Pool, Fine Dining, Yoga, Spa

GUANA

GUANA ISLAND
Private Island, British Virgin Islands
Tel: (800) 544-8262
www.guana.com
Luxury
Beach, Watersports, Tennis, Hiking,
Nature Tours, Yoga

JAMAICA

THE IAN FLEMING VILLA,
GOLDENEYE
Oracabessa, St Mary, Jamaica
Tel: +1 (876) 975-3354
www.islandoutpost.com
Luxury
Private Beach, Pool, Private Chef,
Watersports

ITOPIA
Runaway Bay, Jamaica
Tel: (800) 688-7678
www.islandoutpost.com
Moderate
Historic

KANOPI HOUSE
Blue Lagoon, Port Antonio, Jamaica
Tel: +1 (867) 632-3213
www.kanopihouse.com
Luxury
Private Lagoon Access, Watersports,
Private Chef

ROUND HILL HOTEL
AND VILLAS
Montego Bay, Jamaica
Tel: +1 (876) 956-7050
www.roundhilljamaica.com
Premiere
Beach, Pool, Tennis, Private Chefs in some
Villas, Fine Dining, Gym, Spa

TRYALL CLUB
Sandy Bay, Jamaica
Tel: +1 (876) 956-5660
www.tryallclub.com
Premiere
Beach, Pool, Tennis, Golf,
Private Chefs in Villas, Gym, Spa

MUSTIQUE

AURORA
Mustique, St. Vincent and the Grenadines,
West Indies
Tel: +1 (784) 488-8000
www.mustique-island.com
Luxury
Pool, Private chef

COTTON HOUSE
Mustique, St. Vincent & The Grenadines,
West Indies
Tel: (800) 223-1108
www.cottonhouseresort.com
Premiere
Private Beach, Pool, Tennis, Spa, Gym

FIREFLY
Mustique, St Vincent & The Grenadines,
West Indies
Tel: +1 (784) 488-8414
www.fireflymustique.com
Luxury
Pool

YEMANJÁ
Mustique, St. Vincent and the Grenadines,
West Indies
Tel: +1 (784) 488-8000
www.mustique-island.com
Premiere
Pool, Tennis, Private chef

NEVIS
The Hermitage
Nevis, French West Indies
Tel: +1 (869) 469-3477
www.hermitagenevis.com
Moderate
Pool, Historic

MONTPELIER PLANTATION
Nevis, French West Indies
Tel: +1 (869) 469-3462
www.montpeliernevis.com
Premiere
Pool, Beach Club, Fine Dining

PUERTO RICO

HORNED DORSET
Primavera
Rincón, Puerto Rico
Tel: (800) 633-1857
www.horneddorset.com
Luxury
Pool, Beach, Fine Dining,
Watersports, Spa

ST BARTHS

ISLE DE FRANCE
Baie des Flamands, Saint Barthélemy,
French West Indies
Tel: (59) 05 90 27 61 81
www.isle-de-france.com
Premiere
Pool, Beach, Fine Dining, Tennis, Spa

MAISON NOUREEV
Cote Sauvage, Saint Barthélemy,
French West Indies
Tel: +1 (617) 349-0090
www.noureev.com
Moderate
Historic

LE SERENO
Grand Cul-de-Sac, St Barthélemy,
French West Indies
Tel: +59 (05) 90 29 83 00; (888) 537-3736
www.lesereno.com
Luxury
Pool, Beach, Fine Dining

VILLA LA DANSE
Des Etoiles
Pointe Milou, St Barthélemy,
French West Indies
Tel: (866) 776-2613
www.ladansedesetoiles.com
Premiere
Pool, Private Chef (upon request)

ST. LUCIA

JADE MOUNTAIN
St Lucia, West Indies
Tel: +1 (758) 459-4000
www.jademountain.com
Premiere
Plunge pools, Beach, Fine Dining,
Gym, Spa

LADERA RESORT
St Lucia, West Indies
Tel: +1 (758) 459-6600; +1 (758) 459-7323
www.ladera.com
Luxury
Pool, Beach Access, Fine Dining,
Spa, Gym

PREMIERE: $$$$$
LUXURY: $$$$
MODERATE: $$$

ACKNOWLEDGMENTS

With each Hideaways series book I endeavor to write, I realize how incredibly involved they are and moreover, how they require and rely on the generosity and participation of so many others. Right from the initial research through to the final caption, I am dependent upon other kind souls to carry me through to success. As a result, my list of thanks is far longer than this layout allows. For everyone who graciously responded to an email with "Caribbean Hideaways" emboldened in its subject line, I thank you for helping me along my way. A very special thank you goes to the myriad public relations professionals, sales and marketing directors, and property managers who were the central respondents of such emails and followed up with helpful suggestions, quick answers, and patience with my extremely tight schedule and budget. Without your help (and my sincere apologies that there are too many to name here), this book simply wouldn't exist. I am also beholden to the generous hosts of the selected properties, who make my task not only easier, but also a fantastically rich experience; thank you. A special thank you to Annie Curtin and Hayden Sundin, Jon and Melody Dill, Monica and Walter Noel, Linda Smith, Robert Hew, Kenny of Kenny Tours, Sally Henzell, Chris Blackwell, Richard Friedman, Guillermo Paz, Ed Hamilton and the crews of Genesis and Makayabella, the Tourism Boards of Grenada, Nevis and St. Lucia, Firefly's Elizabeth Bishop, Stiles Bennett at Wimco, Jeanne and Nicolas Audy-Rowland, Etienne van der Nest, and William and Usha Gordon for going above and beyond.

To those whose behind-the-scenes effort ensures the book's ultimate achievement: I would like to thank Peter Goldman at Aporia Inc. for his excellent print work, Elizabeth Smith and Victoria Brown for their invaluable input and necessary corrections; Sara Stemen for her inspiring design and leniency; Claire L. Gierczak for her diligent and tireless assistance; and my wonderfully serene editor, Kathleen Jayes, who belies my dramatic pronouncements with pragmatism and grace. An enormous thank you also goes to Rizzoli International Publications and Charles Miers for permitting me to share my passion in such reputable fashion.

I'd like to thank my fabulous partner-in-crime, Jessica Antola, with the promise of an annual nutmeg-topped rum punch and a toneless, reggae-infused rendition of "Apologize." To my family, who endure my grumpy attitude when the final writing inevitably falls during the summer vacation. And last, I am forever grateful to my husband, Friso van Reesema, whose benevolent nature has allowed me to live my dream of travel while still reaping the benefits of a caring and flourishing partnership.

OPPOSITE PAGE
Serene seating at Aquamare.

FOLLOWING PAGE
Sunset at Tryall.

MEG NOLAN VAN REESEMA

As a travel writer and luxury hotel and villa consultant specializing in boutique properties, van Reesema has stayed in over four hundred hotels and villas in the last three years. She divides her time between Amsterdam and New York, though as the Travel Editor for Plum TV and the author of the popular travel blog, www.wherenextwithmeg.com, she is rarely at home. Previously, she was an editor at *Town & Country* and on staff at *Vanity Fair*. Her work regularly appears in *Town & Country*, *Interiors Magazine*, and *Hotelier International*.

JESSICA ANTOLA

In her decade-long photography career and as an avid traveler, Antola has shot advertising campaigns for globally recognized brands such as American Express, features for international magazines like *Travel + Leisure*, *W*, and *Dwell*, as well as rarely-covered people, cultures, and landscapes from West Papua to Myanmar. Her awards include Photo District News, PDN's 30, The International Photography Awards, and American Photography 24 and 25.